This Journal belongs to:

....

....

....

....

Phone: ....

Email: ....

I know you are busy. However, if you find this Journal, I would be grateful if you could return it to the address above. As a gesture of my appreciation, I will offer a reward of $

THE STRATEGY
JOURNAL

BY KRIS SAFAROVA

CEO of FIRMSconsulting and StrategyTraining.com
Succeeding as a Management Consultant, Author
Turquoise Eyes, Author

FIRMSconsulting LLC

Los Angeles

THE STRATEGY JOURNAL

© 2020 Firmsconsulting LLC
A Kris Safarova | StrategyTraining.com & FIRMSconsulting.com Original
June 2020

Published & Printed in the United States of America by Firmsconsulting LLC,
a member of The Strategy Media Group LLC, Los Angeles.

www.firmsconsulting.com

Firmsconsulting and The Strategy Media Group are registered trademarks of The Strategy Media Group.

Firmsconsulting business books are available at special discounts for bulk purchases for sales promotions or corporate use. Special editions, including personalized covers, excerpts of existing books, or books with corporate logos can be created in large quantities for special needs. For more information please contact **info@firmsconsulting.com**.

All Rights Reserved. This book or parts thereof may not be reproduced in any form, stored in any retrieval system, or transmitted in any form by any means—electronic, mechanical, photocopy, recording, or otherwise—without permission of the publisher, except as provided by United States of America copyright law. For permission requests, write to the publisher, at the address below

FIRMSCONSULTING L.L.C.	THE STRATEGY MEDIA GROUP L.L.C.
187 E. Warm Springs Rd.	8605 Santa Monica Blvd
Suite B158	West Hollywood, CA 90069-4109
Las Vegas, NV 89119	USA
USA	support@firmsconsulting.com
support@firmsconsulting.com	

Disclaimer: This work contains general information only and is not intended to be construed as rendering accounting, business, financial investment, legal, tax, or other professional advice and/or services. This work is not a substitute for such professional advice and services, nor should it be used as a basis for any decision or action that may affect your business and/or career. The author and publisher disclaim any liability, loss, or risk that is incurred as a consequence of the use and applications of any of the contents of this work.

Terms of Use: This is a copyrighted work, and Firmsconsulting LLC companies ("Firmsconsulting") and its licensors reserve all rights in and to the work. Use of this work is subject to these terms. Except as permitted and the right to store and retrieve one copy of the work, you may not reproduce, modify, create derivative works based upon, transmit, distribute, disseminate, sell, publish, or sublicense the work or any part thereof without Firmsconsulting's prior consent. You may use the work for your own noncommercial and personal use. Any other use of the work is strictly prohibited. Your right to use the work may be terminated if you fail to comply with these terms.

Firmsconsulting and its licensors make no warranties as to the accuracy, adequacy, or completeness of the work or results to be obtained from using the work, including any information that can be accessed through the work through hyperlink or otherwise, and expressly disclaim any warranty, expressed or implied, including but not limited to implied warranties of merchantability or fitness for a particular purpose. Under no circumstances shall Firmsconsulting and/or its licensors be liable for any indirect, incidental, special, punitive, consequential, or similar damages that result from the use of or inability to use the work, even if any of them have been advised of the possibility of such damages.

ISBN 978-1-7340327-4-1

THIS BOOK IS DEDICATED TO MY FAMILY.
MAY THERE BE MORE PEOPLE LIKE THEM
IN THE WORLD.

IT IS ALSO DEDICATED TO OUR CLIENTS
AROUND THE WORLD WHO WORK HARD
TO SOLVE MANKIND'S TOUGHEST PROBLEMS.

FIRMSCONSULTING.COM AND
STRATEGYTRAINING.COM

StrategyTraining.com is a curated site, where membership is earned, for professionals who aspire to learn the skills to solve mankind's toughest problems.

Our members hold themselves to the highest professional standards and aspire to make a difference in the world.

Our content, all prepared by former McKinsey, BCG et al. senior partners, includes books, journals, video and audio training programs teaching the thinking, toolkits, methodologies, and advanced skills needed to improve society.

We produce 3 of the top podcast channels in the world for critical thinking.

Strategy Skills

How to Build a Consulting Firm

Case Interviews and Management Consulting

YOU CAN DO THIS

What will you do when the world calls on you to solve it's toughest problems?

KRIS SAFAROVA

THE WORLD needs you to be a critical thinker.

We work with clients in more than 150 countries around the world. From internal strategy consultants to Fortune 500 EVPs to the executive committee members of the world's largest consulting firms. You are holding the Journal we use in all our training programs, and with all our most successful clients. Despite their intellect, responsibilities, and well-earned successes, many share a fear of not being good enough to do the work. Great strategists are not just good enough at the math and numbers. Great strategists do not confuse being quantitative for being analytic, and neither should you. Great strategists observe, take notes, determine what is holding their clients and their organizations back from breakout success, and do the detective work to solve the problem. So should you.

Make this promise to yourself. If you see something, you will say something. If you see something is not working or can be done better, you will speak up and try to determine what is happening. Great strategy comes from curiosity and a hunger to do things better. Great strategists start with the right questions. The analyses come later, but it is not the hardest part. The hardest part is simply having the confidence to admit things can be better and the willingness to speak up as you figure out how to solve the problem.

You do not need an MBA. You do not need to understand business. And you certainly do not need to have graduated from the *right* school. What you need is the desire to make things better and the perseverance to see things through. Life is too short to settle for being a spectator. You have a role to play in your career. This Journal will help you fulfill your destiny.

Promise yourself right here and now that you will use this Journal to make a difference in your career.

WHAT IS STRATEGY CONSULTING

WE DEFINE STRATEGY as choosing the right business objective and the steps to achieve that business objective so that you create relatively more earnings per share than industry peers and the rest of the market, and do it in a sustainable and ethical way. Strategy consulting is the process an external advisor would use to help a client achieve this goal.

You can have a strategy for pricing, operations, implementation, marketing, branding, logistics, maintenance, merchandising, and more. The list is expansive. However, this means that developing a strategy is the process to develop a plan to solve any business and/or organizational problem. Therefore, everyone should understand the underlying analytic and problem-solving process. This Journal is not only useful to business strategy consultants. If you want to develop a pricing strategy, this Journal will work. The same goes for other business problems you are trying to solve. It will work just as well for non-consultants.

Strategy consulting has taken on elitist connotations, but you need not worry about your background, graduating school, or GPA. The process to solve complex business problems from 1st principles can be learned by anyone, and this Journal will teach you how. The tools taught in this Journal cannot be found in any MBA program anywhere in the world. It is exclusively available here and on our training platforms, including StrategyTraining.com and the Strategy Training apps.

Yet, strategy consulting is more than tools. It is about intent and sincerity. It is about caring about your clients' success and caring about their reputation. It is about teaching them to be fair and responsible corporate citizens who create significant profits. As the person helping develop their strategy, you play a critical role in deciding how they will engage the world. If you care about the world and the well-being of its citizens, help your clients develop products, share their profits, and institutionalize business practices that make the world a better place while making them incredibly wealthy.

WHY WE CREATED THIS JOURNAL

WE HAVE BEEN USING THIS JOURNAL diligently over the last few years, both for our own personal use and with our clients. For decades, we have been strategists. In the last 10 years, we published *Succeeding as a Management Consultant*, *The Corporate Strategy and Transformation Program*, *The US Market Entry Strategy Study*, *Follow a Full McKinsey et al. Engagement*, and >39 other programs, distilling the detailed steps needed to solve complex business problems. We produce new episodes every week. From these >6,100 episodes of content and books, we have taught and continue to teach consulting partners, executive committee members of the major consulting firms, Fortune 500 EVPs, entrepreneurs, consultants, government officials, etc. All our teachings use the approach explained in this Journal. We received many requests to make this Journal available, which is why we have published it.

This Journal was created from our years of experience. Our focus on tracking, documenting and analyzing our clients who are using our training has revealed additional, important strategies for solving difficult strategy problems.

I have had the privilege of working with some of the most eminent ex-partners in the history of BCG, McKinsey, Bain et al., as well as talented executives, entrepreneurs, consultants, and senior partners. Many of the latter are our coaching clients.

All clients want answers. They usually want to know the framework or solution to quickly find an answer. Our goal is to teach them the thinking skills we use, so they can develop their own customized analyses, frameworks, and solutions. If the solution to a clients' problems could be found in a textbook, they would not be paying millions of dollars to firms like McKinsey, BCG, etc., to help solve major issues. All the value is in the tailoring—each problem requires a solution tailored to that situation. We teach you to not be dependent on others for your thinking. Instead, we teach you a skill that will pay for itself in generous dividends for years to come. We teach you the skills to solve mankind's toughest problems and, in the process, change your lives and careers. Like that famous aphorism, we do not give you a fish. We teach you how to fish.

This Journal builds on our strategy studies like *Follow a Full McKinsey et al. Engagement* and books like *Succeeding as a Management Consultant* to create a daily tool that can be used to solve any business problem. We focus on measurable financial benefits. It is a step-by-step approach with the templates, guides, and explanations that help you to accomplish what you have seen us do for over 10 years on some of the toughest problems in the world. The Journal summarizes the most important things you need to do and eliminates all the noise from the process.

THE STRATEGY JOURNAL

This is not a diary, calendar, or planner. This is a Journal built for those who want to do the work, for those who want to solve complex business problems. It is a daily tool that helps you ask the right questions, collect the right data, conduct the right analyses, communicate the right findings, influence your colleagues to act, and know what needs to be done at each stage of the study to produce a truly unique solution that solves the original problem. The Journal is there to guide you. It is the tool you will use all the time.

I want you to know this Journal is not a summary of best-practices and unproven anecdotes gleaned from the internet and books. We use scientific rigor in testing the principles, employing strict controls. We know these principles work because we use them every single day. This Journal is the de facto foundation for all the work we do and all the programs you see on StrategyTraining.com + Apps. If you follow the FIRMSconsulting Insider programs, you can see how we use them and follow the results we achieve. We have tracked the results, adjusted the Journal and continue to test the ideas. This Journal is the product of that process.

The Journal has gone through 10 years of iterations. It started with *Succeeding as a Management Consultant* which was published in 2010. Used by many major organizations around the world, the book has had a powerful impact. Afterward, we released the 270+ episode videos, per a study, detailing all the steps to complete difficult strategy assignments. Those were watched by people in over 150 countries. We measured, analyzed, and tracked their usage, and listened to their feedback. We looked at how they used the videos. We realized a Journal they could use to replace their notes and own tools would be ideal. That is why we created this Journal. It went through multiple rounds of iterations—suggested by some of our most successful clients—to test and improve.

Clients who have used the Journal have reported more successful projects, fulfilling careers, happier colleagues, superior recommendations, an improvement in their overall joy and skill levels, and rapid promotions. They cite increased productivity since the Journal keeps them focused on the most important issues and more face-time with clients. They report better results and greater benefits for their clients. They have found a way to numerically quantify the value of their work and place a value on the improvement to their clients. They cite a renewed interest, vigor, and excitement in their work. Many say they, for the first time, believe they are doing something important and making a difference. And this feedback is consistent, all the way from corporate employees to senior partners to business analysts to internal consultants to consultants at boutique firms. We know you can have the same results if you put in the required work.

THE STRATEGY JOURNAL

WHAT YOU WILL FIND

t **HERE ARE 16 TYPES OF PAGES IN THIS JOURNAL:** Project Logic and Overview, Decision-Tree of Options, Hypotheses, Hypotheses Tests, Storyboarding, Charter, Timeline, Flash Report, Focus Interviews, Executive Update Guide, Financial Analyses, Benchmarks, Case Studies, Project Checklist, Opportunity Chart, Benefits Chart and Daily Pages.

The heart of this Journal revolves around the pages to plan your study: from clarifying the problem statement all the way to developing the presentation and quantifying the benefits case in $. The Journal is divided into 3 parts: Overview, Guided Example and Your Study. The Overview offers you a 1-page guide to the entire process we will use to create a highly customized solution for your client. In the Guided Example we will work together through a study/project to show you how each page will be used. Thereafter, we create templates and guides for you to use on your own study.

The Daily Pages are split into 8 weeks with a page for Monday to Friday. The pages help you understand your goals in each day with a timeline reminder of the deliverables before each client update. Reminders for the client updates are built into the sheets for you to complete.

The Journal helps identify, measure and bank the dollar value for your client (or employer) through prompts, templates and steps to follow. If you are unsure of the process, we have built in checks and balances so that you can go back and make corrections to any gaps in your earlier thinking. There are explicit steps and milestones to validate each of your assumptions.

As the study begins to wrap up, we move to implementation. We show you what needs to be done to begin the discussion about implementation, what to implement, and how to measure and track the implementation benefits, including the sale of the implementation program.

The Journal can replace all your primary planning and project management tools. By moving everything to one document that you can use every day and all the time, it allows you to better track and manage the engagement. Slides and updates can be prepared in the journal and shared with your team and clients. By moving from laptop and slide-based discussions with clients, the Journal increases the level of professional intimacy with a client. The Journal is designed to be stored forever. This will contain your best thinking and should serve as a library for future studies.

YOU ARE NOT ALONE

AT THIS VERY MOMENT, I know for a fact that I am using this Journal at the same time it is being used in many studies and by many clients around the world. We are all held together by the common philosophy and tools in this Journal. We start our days in the same way, manage our studies in the same way, and archive our lessons in the same way. We belong to an exclusive shared value system. We created this Journal to level the playing field. We wanted everyone who desired to have an impact in the world to have the very best tools in the world. With that level of support, your results will come down to your initiative, judgment, and creativity. Lack of access to the best thinking and support should not hold you back. We want you to be the best you can be.

The world will remember that you lived, took a stand that mattered, and made a difference.

If you ever need more inspiration or strategies, subscribe to our three iTunes podcast channels and our YouTube channel. If you want to learn advanced strategy problem-solving skills and have access to our most advanced programs, subscribe to FIRMSconsulting.com Premium membership and become a FIRMSconsulting Insider, our earned loyalty level. FIRMSconsulting Insiders unlock access to our advanced training. You can see how we apply this thinking to solving complex strategy problems, building new businesses, helping partners thrive, overcoming career obstacles, and helping boutique firms. And you will learn from the best. The Titans of Strategy series includes eminent ex-McKinsey, BCG senior partners like Kevin P. Coyne and Bill Matassoni teaching the skills they developed advising CEOs around the world. We make these programs available to you to ensure you are not alone in your journey and have access to unique and powerful insights that will help you make a meaningful impact.

Your clients and colleagues need you. Your organization needs you to be your best. You need to be your best for yourself and your family. And you will be the best. You should be proud that you have made this first step to make a difference in the world. You are not alone. We are in this together, and we will develop together. We are using the same playbook. Stick to the plan and follow this Journal. You will see the results in a month; please post them tagging #strategyjournal so we can celebrate with you.

Kris Safarova

VALUES

WE HOPE *you will take the time to read our company values and make them a part of your professional journey, whether you work in a boutique consulting firm, large professional services firm, or within a corporate environment. By having an open, sincere, and positive approach to serving a client, or an organization, you will build a legacy.*

I have chosen to be an advisor. I have asked for the opportunity to serve this client. I understand and respect the trust the client has placed in me. I know that it is not my right to serve this client. It is a privilege, and I will work every day to earn that privilege.

I am not perfect. I will learn new things every day. I will treat this client and opportunity as a chance to discover new and better ways of solving this problem. I will try to make this the most effective study ever done for this problem and help my client be the best they can be.

Not every day is going to be great. Clients are under pressure. Sometimes things will be said in the moment. I will remember it is not personal. I will work to de-escalate the situation and help them through their hour of need.

I know that business is about money. Good intentions cost money. Pursuing social causes costs money. If I want my clients to champion important causes in the world, I must help them make money to afford such initiatives. I will ensure this study ends with the client finding quantifiable and employee-verified benefits that are a client-approved multiple of my fees and implementation costs.

I value my reputation. There will be times when I am unable to help a client or do not agree with a decision they are making. When this happens, I will amicably step aside because I know that it is more important to help a client do what is in their best interests than take a fee for advice that will not help them. When this happens, I will remain on good terms and maintain the relationship.

I will treat the clients' resources as if they were my own. I will always recognize that shareholders are my ultimate clients. I will always take the reasonable path when incurring expenses, such as when purchasing meals the client pays for.

I will enjoy this study and appreciate the impact I am having. I am an artist. I will create unique, powerful, and innovative solutions grounded in logic and facts. I understand there are always better ways to solve every problem. For a smaller client, I am playing a pivotal role in helping them grow. For a larger client, I am helping them become better. It is a wonderful opportunity, and my work will be felt by thousands if not millions of employees, suppliers, and consumers.

I will never disclose my clients' identities or secrets unless they ask me to. I realize clients are sharing sensitive information with me and sharing it in any shape or form without their permission does not help them. It also leads potential clients to question my values.

Building my firm, practice and/or career can be a lonely path. Yet, I know I am not alone because I have the FIRMSconsulting community for support. Advice is just one episode away, and I can get access to over 6,100 training episodes on **StrategyTraining.com**.

Good Thoughts.
Good Actions.
Good Results.

Kris Safarova

SEE THE JOURNAL IN ACTION

Follow an engagement team as they use the tools in this journal to solve a real client problem.

Bill, a former McKinsey and BCG partner, distills his life and lessons in his captivating memoir. Learn about the unique strategy McKinsey deploys to be the most elite consulting firm in the world.

Follow a consulting team over 8-weeks as they help a company diagnose and fix a persistent performance problem. This is the only book of its kind walking the reader step-by-step through a complete consulting study.

Set after a bank begins implementing a new retail banking strategy, we follow Teresa, a director general, who has received some disturbing news. There is a mistake in the loan default calculations and reserve ratios. The numbers do not add up.

START HERE

Analyzing a problem from 1st principles is an exciting process and a powerful skill to learn. The approach we will teach you can be used for strategy, operations, pricing, supply chain, etc., problems. We not only work with eminent ex-McKinsey, BCG et al. partners to develop our training programs, but will show you the approach we teach clients around the world, including executive committee members at the world's largest consulting firms.

First, we will show you the overall process.

Second, we will lead you through an example.

Third, we have templates and daily guides for you to follow to complete your own study.

At the end of each study, keep this Journal. It will contain your finest work.

THE STRATEGY JOURNAL

THE OVERALL APPROACH: REFER TO THIS PAGE THROUGHOUT THE STUDY

This is the overall approach used in all well-managed studies at the most elite firms. It is also the underlying approach. If you follow it diligently, you will produce a highly customized and useful recommendation for the client, with measurable benefits.

You will manage your team more effectively, improve your reputation with your client and produce a verifiable recommendation that can be implemented. This approach ensures your recommendation will produce quantifiable, bankable benefits to the client, and that is the most powerful advantage you can bring to a client, and the most enduring reputation you can have as an advisor.

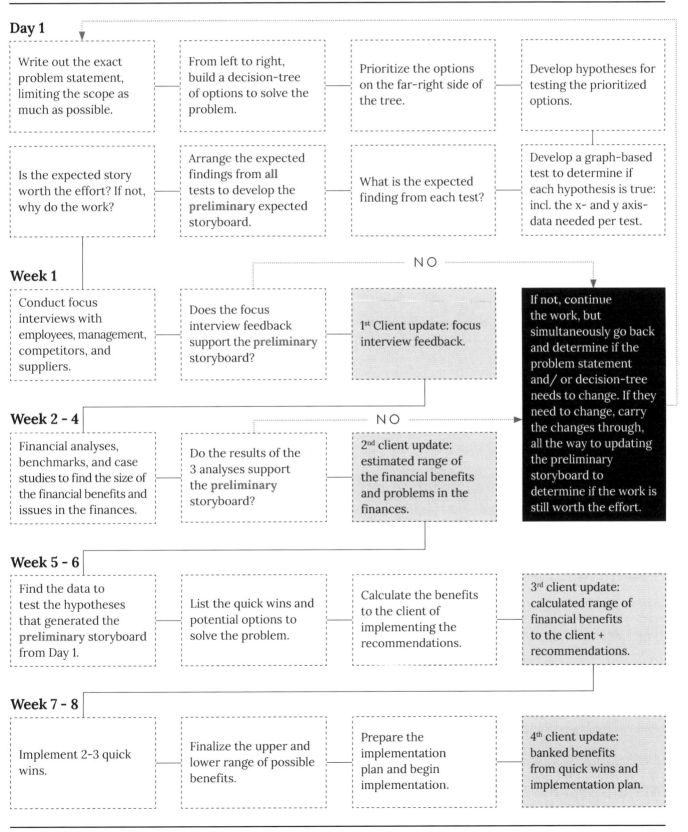

FREE EPISODE FROM BOOK'S COMPANION COURSE AT FIRMSCONSULTING.COM/STRATEGYJOURNAL

A GUIDED EXAMPLE

Now, we will do an example together so you can see how this process works. It can be daunting, but if you diligently follow the process you will produce insightful results for your company, division, and/or client. Your career will be transformed. Critical thinking is a process, and this is the process.

Do not be intimidated by the approach and concepts you will learn. If you do not understand an area, make a note, but complete the entire guided example. Things will make sense as you work through the example. Just go through the steps carefully and trust the process.

You will be tempted to memorize frameworks. Don't do it. Every problem to be solved is unique and requires a unique framework.

PLANNING
day 1 & 2
OF THE STUDY

THE STRATEGY JOURNAL

step 1: BUILD A DECISION TREE OF OPTIONS TO SOLVE THE PROBLEM

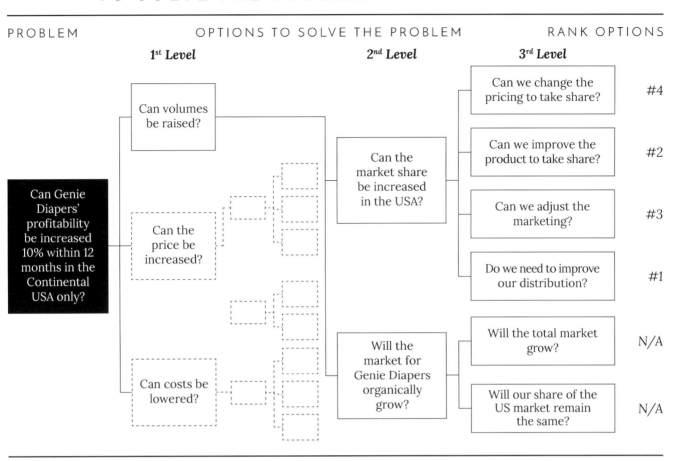

All the planning work in this section happens **before** the study commences. You read that correctly. You can do all this using your existing knowledge of the client and the sector, and business in general. This does not require any research. Just good judgment. Complete this section the day before the study or at the very least during the first two days of the study. It must be done before the work begins. In the pages that follow, we will walk you through each step. You should fight the urge to dive into mountains of research and reading at this stage. You will know enough to complete this step and there are enough checks and balances built into the process to correct any gaps in your thinking. Trust yourself and proceed. This is the process we use in all our studies and the process we ask our clients to use.

THE PROBLEM STATEMENT is the main part. If you get this wrong, you could have the best analysis, but will end up solving the wrong problem. You must be as specific as possible to narrow the scope of the problem. Keep rewriting the problem statement to include the metric that measures success, the numerical target you are trying to hit for this metric, the timeframe to solve the problem, and the scope of products and regions covered. This will help prevent scope creep later.

THE OPTION TREE is the process of listing the options to fix the problem. Here you will use the concept of MECE (Mutually Exclusive/Collectively Exhaustive). Collectively exhaustive means you have listed all the options to fix a branch of the decision tree. Mutually exclusive means one option can be implemented, while keeping the others unchanged. In the example above, we built out the option tree for raising volume. We would also do this for pricing and costs. In your study, you should build out all the branches that are important. You can see we went down to the 3rd level of branches from left to right. You should build out your decision tree to the 3rd or 5th level. Anything more is usually not useful this early.

PRIORITIZING the branches/options on the far right is the final step. You will prioritize the branches by deciding which option will lead to the problem being solved and solved the fastest. This is important because testing each branch to see if it will solve the problem takes time and money. You want to start with the branch most likely to solve the problem, so you save the client time and money.

THE STRATEGY JOURNAL

step 2: DEVELOP YOUR HYPOTHESES FOR THE PRIORITIZED OPTIONS

HYPOTHESES

#1 Do we need to improve our distribution?

Due to the lack of a functioning ecommerce site, Genie Diapers is wholly dependent on retail stores, which leads to lower sales among millennials.

#2 Can we improve the product to take share?

Due to a lack of waterproof tape fasteners, customers prefer more expensive competitors, which leads to a loss of value and volume share.

#3 Can we adjust the marketing?

Due to cost cuts over the last 2 years Genie Diapers has pulled all TV and print advertisements, which has led to loss of mindshare among customers.

#4 Can we change the pricing to take share?

Due to having among the lowest marginal costs of production, Genie Diapers can lower prices, which would lead to a gain in market share while remaining profitable.

#5 Will the total market grow?

N/A

#6 Will our share of the US market remain the same?

N/A

For each of the options you prioritized (black block on the left) write out a hypothesis (perforated block on the left). A hypothesis is your understanding of how this option will fix the problem and the consequences thereafter.

Hypotheses should have 3 parts to make them easy to test.

Due to x…
…y happens…
…which leads to z…

Create a hypothesis for each of the options you prioritized and in the order you prioritized them.

We have decided not to test branches #5 and #6 since they will not solve the problem for us. This means you should not test every option, just the prioritized ones.

In your study you will almost certainly have more options and hypotheses. Expect to have between 8 and 15 good hypotheses.

THE STRATEGY JOURNAL

step 3: DESIGN YOUR ANALYSES TO TEST THE HYPOTHESES

Now we must design the analysis to test each hypothesis. The testing of the analyses is what many consider to be the main work consultants do. It is not, but it is a large part of the work. For each hypothesis, think of the test you would conduct to determine if the hypothesis is true. Go as far as sketching out the exhibit you would plot, with the data you would collect. Include the x- and y-axis in your exhibit. This is important since it will guide your data needs later. Complete the exhibit by hand with the approximate/best-guess data you expect to find. Do not start collecting the data just yet.

In each of our hypotheses we needed to do two tests. For example, in the hypothesis for option #1 below, the first test is an exhibit to show Genie Diapers sales by channel to see the size of e-commerce sales. The second is an exhibit to show the fastest growing consumer segments by their preferred channel.

Each analysis tests the entire hypothesis or part of a hypothesis. You can test a hypothesis with 1, 2, or even 3 tests. Given the way we wrote the hypotheses with 2 parts, usually 2 tests will work. Each test is placed on a separate PowerPoint slide. As we place the PowerPoint slides together, we are building out our presentation. Use different types of graphs for each slide, from bar charts to pie charts to rankings of the frequency of an item coming up in focus interviews. Remember, all the work in this section should be completed in a day or two at most. Strategy studies are fast-paced and focused, but trust the process.

CONVERT THE HYPOTHESES... ...INTO ANALYSES TO TEST THEM

#1 Do we need to improve our distribution?

Due to the lack of a functioning ecommerce site, Genie Diapers is wholly dependent on retail stores, which leads to lower sales among millennials.

analysis for **distribution**

#2 Can we improve the product to take share?

Due to a lack of waterproof tape fasteners, customers prefer more expensive competitors, which leads to a loss of value and volume share.

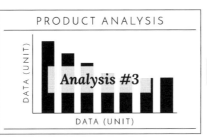

analysis for **product**

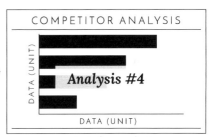

analysis for **product**

#3 Can we adjust the marketing?

Due to cost cuts over the last 2 years Genie Diapers has pulled all TV and print advertisements, which has led to loss of mindshare among customers.

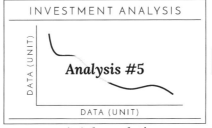

analysis for **marketing**

analysis for **marketing**

#4 Can we change the pricing to take share?

Due to having among the lowest marginal costs of production, Genie Diapers can lower prices, which would lead to a gain in market share while remaining profitable.

analysis for **pricing**

analysis for **pricing**

THE STRATEGY JOURNAL

step 4: BUILD, REFINE AND TEST YOUR PRELIMINARY STORYBOARD

In step 3, we showed you how each analysis to test your prioritized hypotheses becomes the slides in your presentation. The x- and y-axis in the graphs in each slide become your data needs. We still must determine if this is worth all the effort. A good consultant will determine if an analysis is worth the effort to find the data *before* finding the data.

STORYBOARDS help us determine if the analyses we have designed are worth the effort. If we finish the *preliminary* storyboard and determine the story is not riveting, compelling, and worthwhile for the client to implement, we must ask ourselves if this is worth doing at all. You should discuss the story with the client to gain his or her initial views. You can share this storyboard with your team. You should share this with your manager/partner to see if they think you are bringing a compelling message to the study. Build the storyboard by taking the headline from each slide on the previous page. Keep editing each headline until the headline, by itself, allows you to understand what is on that single slide without having to read the slide.

You may have to edit the headlines several times. At the end, you will have a headline that tells the story of that single slide. Once you have done that, rearrange the order of all the headlines from all the slides to tell a story. And when all the headlines are read together, they tell the complete story. See how we improved the story below through several rounds of changes, until we have the final story, where we rearranged the order of the headlines to tell a better story. The questions at the end of the page help you determine if this is worth the effort. If the story is not worth it, either you are not finding enough benefits, or the problem is not really as bad as you thought it was.

BUILDING YOUR STORYBOARD

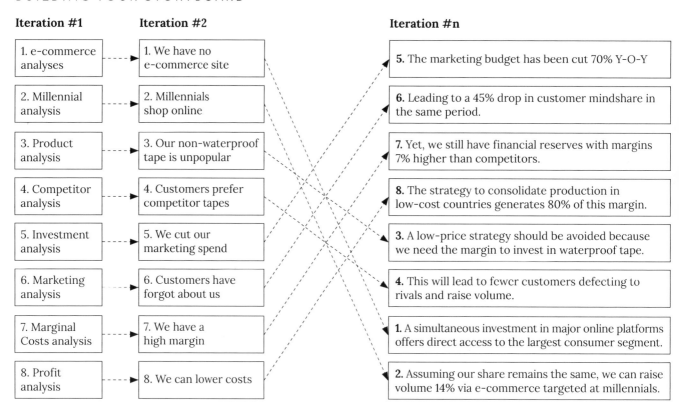

THE STRATEGY JOURNAL

step 5: FINISH YOUR STORYBOARD AKA ANALYSES PLAN

Insert those improved and rewritten headlines (step 4) back into the headlines in the slides (step 3). For each analysis, you will have something that looks like the examples at the bottom of this page: A set of slides with headlines and handwritten diagrams of the analyses we expect to complete.

Can you see what we did? We went from:
Problem statement...
...to decision tree of options...
...to prioritized options...
...to hypotheses for prioritized options...
...to tests for hypotheses...
...to slides for each test...
...to refined headlines for each slide...
...to a preliminary storyboard (and analyses plan) by rearranging the slides.

Congratulations! This is your analytic work plan. It is your list of activities to do on the study. Rather than conducting Google searches for increasing diaper profits or copying the approach used by another consulting firm, you have developed your own customized analysis plan for the client. You now know all the primary analyses you will need to complete over the duration of the study and can plan your time, resources, etc. You can even decide staffing with this.

You can start the analysis now. Yet, all the work completed thus far remains a highly educated and well-structured guess. All of this was done in about 1 to 2 days before you have started the study. The next step is to see if your problem statement and storyboard capture the real issues of the client. We call this the validation steps, and it is explained on the pages that follow. Only once we have finished the validation steps do we start and thereafter present the finished analyses.

ANALYSIS / PRELIMINARY STORYBOARD

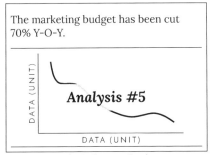
analysis for **marketing**

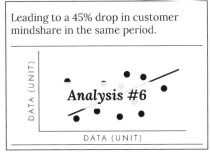
analysis for **marketing**

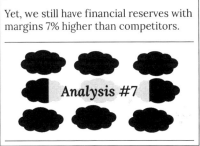
analysis for **pricing**

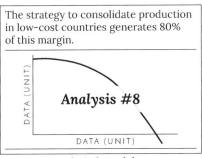
analysis for **pricing**

analysis for **product**

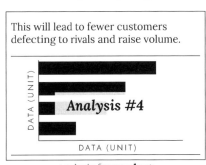
analysis for **product**

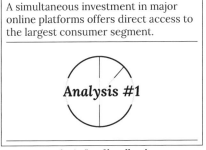
analysis for **distribution**

analysis for **distribution**

TOOLS TO HELP THE CLIENT AND YOUR TEAM

———

A client is, however, usually able and willing to approve a 1-month extension to the current project, especially with a reduced team where the objectives and benefits of the 1-month extension are clear: implementing quick wins while the benefits are being validated by their own employees, who are enthusiastic about the work.

THE STRATEGY JOURNAL

step 6: DEVELOP YOUR CHARTER

This should be done *after* step 5 and *before* step 11, the focus interviews. This usually means completing this section on Day 1 or 2 of Week 1. The charter is your "contract" with your client and team on a day-to-day basis. Use this document in your Journal to manage scope creep and guide the client and your teams. It is a snapshot of everything that needs to be done.

Objectives	Key Activities	Deliverables
• Answer the "what" of your analyses. • There should be no more than 3 or 4 objectives at most.	• Arrange chronologically. • List both intangible and tangible activities. • Focus on the big buckets of activities or significant sub-deliverables. • Think of it as the critical path, the bucket of activities that MUST be done to complete the study.	• A deliverable can be both a question you are answering or major piece of analysis. • The question is useful to the client, while the analyses helps the manager understand how you will do the work. • There are rarely more than 4 or 5 major deliverables.
Scope		**Critical Success Factors**
• List the option(s) being analyzed. • List scenarios being tested. • Set limits to geographies, divisions, products, etc. • Never set limits to analyses types. Set limits to objectives or options. • Do not set limits to the depth of the study – it confuses the client. • Best written as "what is included" versus "what is excluded."		• Focus on your 5 major stakeholders: client, team, manager, partner on the study, and the firm. • List only the most important obstacles they need to help you overcome. • Think of this as a "I told you so" document.

FINISHED CHARTER

Objectives	Key Activities	Deliverables
• Determine how to increase Genie Diapers profits by 10% within 12 months in the Continental USA. • Calculate the net benefits and payback period of the recommendations.	• Expectations exchange with CFO/manager to agree on deliverables. • Identify key stakeholder groups. • Develop problem statement, structure, and hypotheses for the study and get buy-in. • Identify key information requirements to run the analyses. • Develop focus interviews. • Conduct interviews. • Conduct financial analyses, high-level benchmarking and case studies to understand drivers/levers of profits. • Source/facilitate the finding of information. • Guide team and client. • Manage options analyses and recommendation processes. • Develop key decision criteria for option selection. • Build simple model to estimate net benefit of preferred option. • Develop recommendations on optimal option and scenario.	• Current performance of Genie Diapers. • Drivers of profitability. • Benefits case for the preferred option. • Implementation plan. • Quick wins list.
Scope		**Critical Success Factors**
• Top-down business case on the net benefits. • Only Continental USA. • Only the diapers product. • Assumes factory operations not part of the diaper division. • Assumes all data provided by Genie Diapers is accurate. • 4 main options to analyze: product, price, promotion and channels.		• Client commitment. • Timely access to key personnel and the CFO. • Timely access to key external stakeholders. • Timely access to information. • Accurate data. • Clear, open, and honest communication between all stakeholders.

THE STRATEGY JOURNAL

step 7: DEVELOP YOUR PROJECT LOGIC

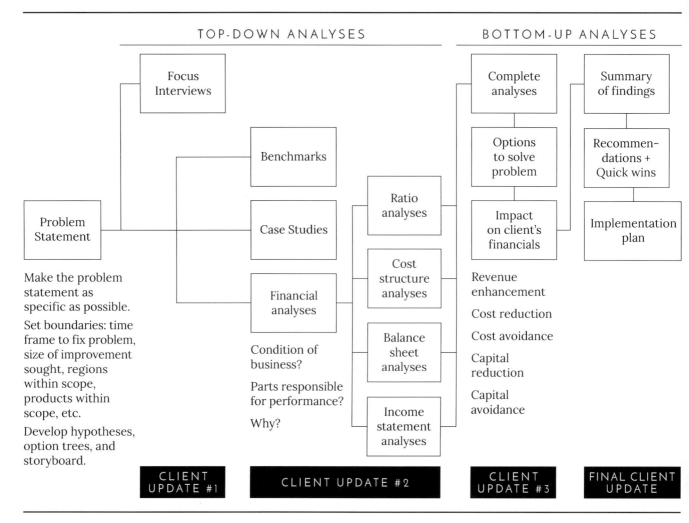

All studies follow the same analytical approach. Use this project logic. Following this approach will not lead to cookie-cutter solutions since the data, analyses, and the way you interpret information and recommend solutions to a client will always be different from another consultant and/or firm. Your client updates are divided into 4 parts.

CLIENT UPDATE #1 always begins with the focus interviews, which help you inform the client what employees, suppliers, and/or stakeholders think about the issue being fixed, the reasons the issue exists, and what can be done to solve the problem. You may find other pressing problems worth raising with the client but think about how they will impact your current study. Do not bring them up until you are certain you understand how to manage the discussion.

CLIENT UPDATE #2 estimates the size of the prize for the client and identifies problems in the financials. Assuming the problems were fixed, how much financial gain would the client see? This step is important for both the client and consultant because the fees and effort to fix the problem should be orders of magnitude less than the benefits attained by fixing the problem.

CLIENT UPDATE #3 confirms the estimates on the size of the prize from the last update session. You will present the analyses here that you planned **before**, in the first few days, and have now completed. Your analyses will confirm the problem, why it exists, and what could potentially be done to fix the problem, including benefits that can be achieved very quickly with little to no investment (quick wins). The total benefits, *aka* size of the prize, will be traced to changes in the client's financial statements. Since there is always more than one way to fix a problem, list the options and the trade-offs for each.

CLIENT UPDATE #4 presents the plan for the client to bank the benefits you have calculated and the results of implementing 2 or 3 quick wins. If you estimated benefits of $20M from fixing the problem, this update should lay out the investment required from the client, resources from the client and consultant (if necessary), the payback period, and the rate of return for the client. You should have started the implementation work before this final update so that the client can hear real feedback on what you have accomplished so far.

THE STRATEGY JOURNAL

step 8: ADAPT YOUR TIMELINE AND SET MILESTONES

WEEK 0 + 1	WEEK 2	WEEK 3	WEEK 4	WEEK 5	WEEK 6	WEEK 7	WEEK 8
	Update 1			**Update 2**		**Update 3**	**Update 4**
Charter ☐				Finish hypotheses testing ☐		Implement quick wins ☐	
Timelines ☐				Develop opportunities ☐		Bank benefits ☐	
Project logic ☐				Convert opportunities to benefits ☐		Finalize the size of the prize ☐	
Expectations exchange ☐				Validate the size of the prize ☐		Implementation plan ☐	
Hypotheses ☐	Financial analyses		☐	Identify quick wins ☐			
Storyboard ☐	Benchmarks		☐	Validate problems ☐			
Focus interview prep ☐	Case studies		☐	Options to address problems ☐			
	Range of the size of the prize		☐				
Knowledge capture planning ☐	Start testing hypotheses		☐				

It is very rare for a study to last more than eight weeks. In some cases, they may extend to ten weeks, but all studies solving a problem, be they strategy, marketing, digital, operations, pricing, logistics, etc., can be completed in eight to ten weeks. Provided this approach is followed diligently, more time will rarely improve the quality of the recommendations. Given the high fees and disruption to a client's business, consultants should be as efficient as possible. We will use this timeline and checklist to track your progress through your own studies.

The EXPECTATIONS EXCHANGE is a meeting, guided by a bullet point list of the five to ten things you need from your manager/direct report and vice versa. This is an important step to ensure there are no miscommunications about how you prefer to work. Keep the list functional and practical. Think about the things you need to do your best work.

THE STRATEGY JOURNAL

step 9:   PREPARE YOUR WEEKLY TEAM UPDATES

OBJECTIVE	SCHEDULE	TEMPERATURE LAST WEEK	TEMPERATURE THIS WEEK
Can Genie Diaper's profitability be increased 10% within 12 months for Continental USA?	On Schedule *week 1*	Normal	Positive

Consultant: Rajiv Chopra, Analytics Consulting
Client: Genie Diapers, US Division, Diaper Business Unit
Sponsor: Doug Smith, EVP Paper
Champion: Jessica Chen, SVP Strategy
Client Team Member: Namath Kahn, Business Analyst

ACCOMPLISHMENTS
Completed charter
Completed project logic
Completed project timeline
Completed income statement ratio analyses
All focus interviews completed
1st draft focus interview storyboard completed
2 Opportunities identified

KEY ISSUES
Finding diaper competitor margin data
Obtaining wholesale diaper volumes

IMPLEMENTATION ISSUES
Fully understanding the costs behind all e-commerce options
Understanding Amazon transport costs

KEY NEXT STEPS….FROM TODAY

WHAT	WHO	WHEN
Contact P Wang about margin data	GH	12 June
Contact D Smith about wholesale volumes	GH	12 June
Plan team dinner	TN	14 June

KEY NEXT STEPS….FROM PREVIOUS MEETING

WHAT	WHO	WHEN
None – 1st meeting today		

Concern   Normal   Positive

This single-page report is the document each member of the consulting team prepares at the end of the week for the weekly team meeting. This is the ideal way to share ideas, progress, and problems you are experiencing. It takes no more than 10 minutes to prepare and ensures everyone is sharing ideas. Although it is not designed to be shared with clients, it routinely is used this way and will work just as well in that capacity. Just remember that some things you discuss with your team may be premature / inappropriate to discuss with the client. When using the weekly report templates, color in the progress blocks at the top with a marker. The sheet should be shared the morning of the meeting, which is usually a Friday, meaning it should be completed early Friday morning or late Thursday night. Each person should spend 5-10 minutes discussing their sheet and taking any questions. This is a chance to get what you want from your team.

IMPLEMENTATION ISSUES is the section where you capture all the problems you think will become an issue during implementation. If you are working in a team, you can change this to INTEGRATION ISSUES to discuss any problems working with your consulting colleagues.

PREPARING
FOR THE
1ST CLIENT UPDATE

week 1

OF THE STUDY

step 10: OVERALL APPROACH: VALIDATION + ANALYSES

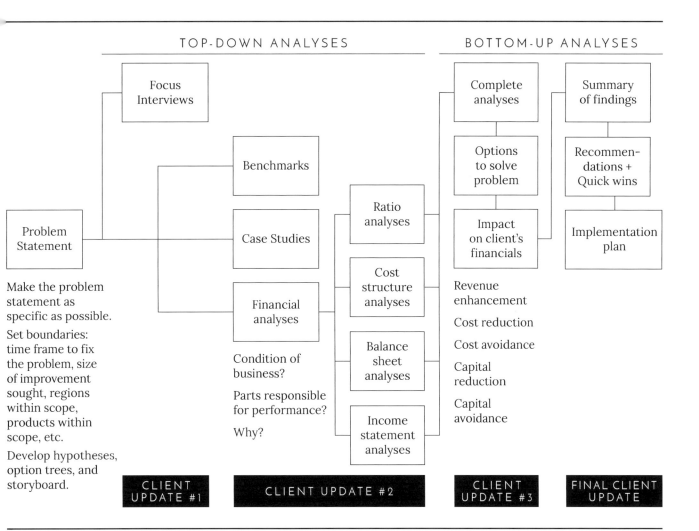

TOP-DOWN analysis always launches the study. Focus interviews, financial analyses, benchmarks, and case studies will tell you what is possible, without explaining why it is possible. The goal of the top-down analysis is to determine the possible financial benefits by identifying **opportunities**. This process helps you decide if the study is worth the effort to proceed. For example, if a cost benchmarking exercise indicates that competitors have 22% lower labor costs and the best performing competitors have 35% lower labor costs, it would seem there is an *opportunity* to lower labor costs. At best, you can estimate the savings by lowering labor costs by 35%. You can also calculate the estimated savings if you think lowering labor costs by 10% is more realistic. If the savings from lowering labor costs by 10% are not worth the effort, you can decide if this is a benefit you want to analyze further. On the other hand, if the labor cost analysis shows you are in line with peers, you know there is probably no benefit there. There may be, but you would need to do something different from those peers. You will collect a list of opportunities giving you a total of the net benefits after the cost of implementation.

BOTTOM-UP analysis validates the top-down analysis by examining the client's numbers, operations, systems, and processes to determine if the 10% labor savings is even possible. The benefit may not be possible, it may be possible, or you may even find bigger and/or new opportunities. You will work with respected client employees to review your assumptions, calculations, and planned implementation approach. If they agree with you, the opportunity becomes a **benefit** and you can use this number to quantify the total benefits for the client. Bottom-up analyses always come at the end.

step 11: PREPARE THE FOCUS INTERVIEWS: SOLE CONTENT FOR THE 1ST EXECUTIVE UPDATE

The focus interviews are divided into two parts. Broad questions (white blocks) to find issues other than what you identified in your decision tree. Variations of questions in the white blocks should be used in every engagement. Those hypotheses that *can* be tested in the focus interviews (grey blocks) *should* be tested in the focus interviews. Interview executives, employees, suppliers, and competitors.

COMPANY PERFORMANCE

Is the company profitable?

Is the company as profitable as it could be?

What has been the general trend for revenue, costs and profits?

Why do you believe it has performed the way it has?

What should be the top 5 priorities to improve performance?

How would you rank these 5 priorities?

Do you believe costs are under control? Why?

MARKET STRUCTURE

What are the major product segments?

What are the needs for each segment?

How well are we meeting the needs? Rank us out of 5, alongside competitors.

Are there any segments not being served well?

For those segments with unmet needs, can they ever be served?

Is the company serving its segments to the best of its ability?

What successes and failures have you had, and what do you ascribe these to?

CUSTOMERS

Who are the primary customers of the business?

What are their top 5 needs?

Can you rank these 5 needs?

Are they served to the best of the company's ability?

What successes and/or failures have we had serving customers?

Are there customers we are not serving with unmet needs?

COMPETITORS

Who are our direct and indirect competitors?

Can you rank them in order of success?

If we added your company to the ranking, where would it go?

Are competitors doing anything better/worse to serve customers than your company is?

Do our competitors have the same business model?

What new innovations have competitors released in the last 3 years?

How have we responded to these innovations?

Have we responded to the best of our ability?

What more could we do? Priorities?

CULTURE

What words would you use to describe the culture of the company?

Can you rank that list in order of most applicable to least applicable?

Has the culture improved or deteriorated?

Why did you provide the answer above?

Are there opportunities to improve the culture?

What changes would you like to see if you could introduce them?

INVESTMENTS

What investments are being made for the long-term?

Do you believe these are the correct investments?

Do you believe the investments are enough?

What do you think should be the priorities?

How would you rank these priorities?

DUE TO A LACK OF A FUNCTIONING E-COMMERCE SITE, GENIE DIAPERS IS WHOLLY DEPENDENT ON RETAIL STORES, WHICH LEADS TO LOWER SALES AMONG MILLENNIALS.

Do we have an e-commerce presence?

Does it impact the company's performance in any way?

Would you change your answer in the top 5 priorities to include this?

What would be the reason for investment in e-commerce?

DUE TO A LACK OF WATERPROOF TAPE FASTENERS, CUSTOMERS PREFER MORE EXPENSIVE COMPETITORS, WHICH LEADS TO A LOSS OF VALUE AND VOLUME SHARE.

Are our products inferior to competitors in any way?

Can you cite specific examples?

How has this impacted the business w.r.t. sales and serving customers?

How do customers respond to our tape fasteners?

Have they offered any suggestions?

DUE TO COST CUTS OVER THE LAST 2 YEARS, GENIE DIAPERS HAS PULLED ALL TV AND PRINT ADVERTISEMENTS, WHICH HAS LED TO LOSS OF MINDSHARE AMONG CUSTOMERS.

Do we have the right amount to spend on marketing?

Where do we advertise?

How should we prioritize our marketing channels?

DUE TO HAVING AMONG THE LOWEST MARGINAL COSTS OF PRODUCTION, GENIE DIAPERS CAN LOWER PRICES, WHICH WOULD LEAD TO GAIN IN MARKET SHARE WHILE REMAINING PROFITABLE.

What is our pricing strategy?

Is it consistently implemented?

Are our margins healthy?

How would you rank our margins against competitors?

THE STRATEGY JOURNAL

step 12: PREPARE THE SLIDES FOR THE 1ST CLIENT EXECUTIVE UPDATE

EXTRACT THE TOP 2 MESSAGES PER FOCUS INTERVIEW SECTION

COMPANY PERFORMANCE

Profits have fallen due to creeping overhead costs, while pricing has remained steady.

85% of managers believe the company is addressing the wrong priorities to restore profitability.

DISTRIBUTION

100% of interviewees believe e-commerce is at least as important as retail.

Although there was disagreement on whether to work with Amazon or build an internal e-commerce capability.

MARKET STRUCTURE

The majority agree that millennials are the fastest growing and most important segment.

90% of managers believe the segment is not served well either by us or competitors.

PRODUCT

Interviewees agree on introducing a waterproof tape.

Yet, they believe this can be outsourced versus being developed internally.

CUSTOMERS

We work with all major retailer/distributors across the country, except Amazon.

We have no product variations for non-bulk online shipping despite retailer requests.

MARKETING

All interviewees believe marketing is a critical investment that should be increased.

Yet, they were divided on what percentages should go to digital, print, and TV.

COMPETITORS

Amazon is widely seen as our main competitor in non-premium diapers and as a channel.

98% of interviewees believe we have not adequately responded to competitor packaging innovations.

PRICING

90% of interviewees believe the pricing is a fair reflection of the product advantages.

Although, they believed more investment must be made in the product to sustain the margins.

CULTURE

There is unanimous agreement the culture has deteriorated as profits have stalled.

Interviewees believe management has ignored the e-commerce trend and stifled e-commerce initiatives.

INVESTMENTS

82% of interviewees believe the production investments have created an enormous competitive advantage.

Though an equal number believe this advantage works best in e-commerce, where we have no presence.

If the focus interviews identify problems/solutions that contradict your problem statement, issues, and hypotheses, DO NOT go ahead with testing those hypotheses. It is expensive to waste time on analyses that do not solve the problem. Wait for the rest of the top-down analyses to be completed to determine if the focus interviews are correct or your initial hypotheses are correct. Focus interviews are rarely incorrect.

WHAT HAPPENS NEXT

Keep refining each message on the left. Expect it to take a few rounds of edits.

Change the order of the messages to create a compelling overall story.

Each message becomes the headline of a single slide.

The body of each slide will be created from the focus interview responses supporting the headline. Use a mix of charts, tables and quotes. However, keep the slides simple, with just one exhibit per slide.

This slide deck becomes the update for your first executive update.

Start studies with focus interviews for 3 reasons:

1. It is difficult for clients to dispute feedback from their own employees. It is factual and builds your credibility from the first presentation because you cannot be told you are wrong in the very first update to the client.

2. You can test if other issues need to be examined, you missed anything important, or you completely misjudged the issues in your earlier hypotheses.

3. Finish the focus interviews within 1 week to gain rapid validation of the direction you are taking. Focus interviews are a quick way to see if your analyses plan is looking at the right issues.

THE STRATEGY JOURNAL

step 13: THE 1ST EXECUTIVE UPDATE

SECTIONS IN THE UPDATE

WHERE WE ARE

Show 4 slides
1. Slide: Problem statement + tree
2. Slide: Timeline
3. Slide: Charter
4. Slide: 3 most important messages you will deliver today. This is your executive summary

WHAT WE FOUND IN FOCUS INTERVIEWS: BROAD SECTION

Show 6-10 slides
1. Tell a story
2. Don't cover every section unless it is part of the story

WHAT WE FOUND IN FOCUS INTERVIEWS: HYPOTHESES TESTED

Show 4-6 slides
1. Tell a story
2. Don't cover every section unless it is part of the story
3. Raise issues that will be addressed in future updates

ASK THE CLIENT TO AGREE TO A DECISION

Show 1 slide
1. Now that we know x and y are not causing the problem to as large a degree, do we agree to focus on z?

WHAT YOU WILL SEE NEXT

Show 1 slide
1. The initial upper/lower benefit range
2. Financial analyses
3. Benchmarks
4. Case Studies

WHAT HAPPENS NEXT

Clients should not see the update slides for the first time in a group client update meeting. If they do, the update becomes a session where the client tries to understand the information and is unable to decide anything. Set up time before the update to explain the slides to them, called pre-presenting, so the updates become decision-making sessions. **To pre-present, the slides must be ready days before the final presentation.** This means the study must be managed in such a way that only minor updates are required to the slides the night before the presentation.

In most cases the focus interviews will identify other equally important problems to fix, and this could become additional billings for you. In some cases you may find a bigger problem to fix than the one you are working on. The first update, therefore, could become an opportunity to confirm the problem statement, or change it if needed.

> Studies typically start with a large set of issues to consider and are continually narrowing the scope of work to focus only on the issues causing the problem. Therefore, every update meeting is NOT just an update. It is a moment for the client to make a decision to narrow the scope. An update meeting where the scope is not narrowed is a wasted opportunity to focus the analyses.

Do you notice we are not starting, finishing, or presenting our core analyses from steps 4 and 5? It is never done upfront. The focus interviews are the first of two validation steps.

Consulting studies cost clients millions of dollars in fees and more when employee time contributions to the consulting engagement are included. Therefore, before starting the bottom-up analyses, it is in everyone's interest to answer two questions upfront:

Are we focusing on the right problem?

Is it worth the effort to solve this problem? This is *aka* "What is the size of the prize?"

The focus interviews answer a large part of the two questions, and the next step, the second client update, will complete answering these two questions.

> In every update, the client will almost certainly ask for additional analyses. Go back to the option tree to see if the work requested helps to solve the original problem statement. If the problem statement and decision tree are correctly constructed, the additional work is probably unnecessary, and you can use the tree to explain why it is unnecessary. If the additional analysis does not help to test the hypotheses, it should not be done.

PREPARING FOR THE 2ND CLIENT UPDATE

week 2 to 4
OF THE STUDY

THE STRATEGY JOURNAL

step 14: BEGIN TWO TYPES OF ANALYSES

ACTIVITY 1: RANGE OF BENEFITS

The 3 analyses below serve two purposes: they offer a rough estimate of the potential benefits from fixing the problem, **and** they validate that you are fixing the right problem. For example, if the financial analyses show significant labor costs, this may be the issue to fix to raise overall company profitability *rather* than trying to raise revenue for the Genie Diapers brand.

The 3 analyses are not intended to solve the problem nor explain the root of the problem. They identify the likely problem. Case studies offer the client real-life examples of peers in similar circumstances.

FINANCIAL ANALYSES

Focus on just a few areas. There is no need for complicated work since the problems will show up in basic analyses:

- Trend analyses
- Ratio analyses
- Income statement
- Balance sheet
- Cash flow statement

Examine items specific to the hypotheses.

BENCHMARKS

Find data for 1 or 2 competitors for most of the above financial analyses.

Competitors may use different methods to calculate the numbers they make available.

By focusing on a few ratios, you have time to adjust them as needed.

CASE STUDIES

Present 3 case studies that are specific to an issue.

For example, present a case study on the problems another company had in entering the e-commerce channel.

It is best to contact past/current employees and interview them versus summarizing internet articles/existing case studies.

ACTIVITY 2: SOLVING THE PROBLEM/TESTING HYPOTHESES

The output from these analyses is NOT presented in the 2nd client update. However, we start this activity now, in the second week, since it can take a long time to complete.

Take the preliminary storyboard you created from the problem statement.

The analyses are straightforward. Find real data to complete the exhibits within the slides.

If the data cannot be found, consider changing the exhibit to test the hypothesis in a different way with different data.

Once all the tests are done, check if the headlines are valid and/or change them based on the real data within the updated exhibits.

If a test raises more relevant questions, conduct more analyses, but only as much as needed to test the hypothesis and solve the original problem.

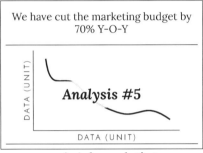
analysis for **marketing**

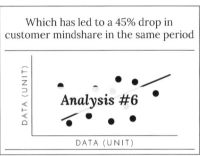
analysis for **marketing**

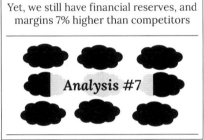
analysis for **pricing**

analysis for **pricing**

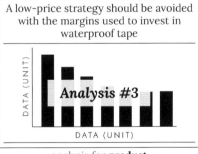
analysis for **product**

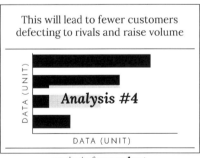
analysis for **product**

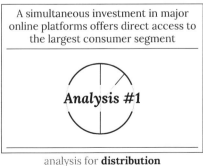
analysis for **distribution**

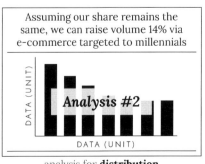
analysis for **distribution**

THE STRATEGY JOURNAL

step 15: COMPLETE THE FINANCIAL ANALYSES

#1 WHAT IS THE CONDITION OF THE BUSINESS?
#2 WHICH PARTS ARE RESPONSIBLE?

Like the focus interviews, you will divide this into two parts: broad examination of the business (#1 and #2) and specific data (#3 on the right) for the problem you are solving.

You want to do this for two reasons: First, if the analyses identify other larger problems the client should deal with them first. Second, part of your role is to identify additional problems that the client should fix. This is how you build your relationship with the client and generate billings.

Focus on a few metrics and always look for data over a few years to show trends. Don't use obscure or complicated analyses. The problems are rarely hidden. Good strategy comes from properly interpreting the numbers *everyone* else can access and has *already* seen.

You need not have the reasons for the problems you identify, nor do you need to verify them at this point. Almost all this information can be provided by the client. Lack of a business background should not deter you. The value you add is by connecting the pieces and asking, for example, why are sales increasing as profits are decreasing? You do not need a finance background nor an MBA to do this. Just be inquisitive and ask questions that arise from what you see.

PROFITS
Return on sales:
Profit margin
Gross margin
Return on net assets
Return on equity

CASH ON HAND
Current ratio
Working capital

SOLVENCY
Debt equity ratio

INVESTMENTS
Price-earning ratio
Earning per share

OVERALL
Costs breakdown

PRODUCT
Return on sales:
Profit margin
Gross margin
Sales
Volume
Pricing

REGION
Return on sales:
Profit margin
Gross margin
Sales
Volume
Pricing

#3 WHAT IS HAPPENING IN THE AREAS HYPOTHESIZED TO BE THE PROBLEM?

You already know what information you need for this part. Now you need to find the information.

See the previous page where we listed the preliminary storyboard with the analyses we will conduct, the exhibit we will plot when we finish the analyses, and the data needed to conduct the analyses.

Can you find any of this data that you need in the financial analyses? If the answer is yes, collect it at this stage of the study.

> PRICING HYPOTHESIS: Due to having among the lowest marginal costs of production Genie Diapers can lower prices, which would lead to gain in market share while remaining profitable.

Need price and market share trends

Need competitor price and market share trends

> PRODUCT HYPOTHESIS: Due to a lack of waterproof tape fasteners, customers prefer more expensive competitors, which leads to a loss of value and volume share.

Need product improvement rollout schedule and market share changes

Need competitor product improvement rollout schedule and market share changes

> MARKETING HYPOTHESIS: Due to cost cuts over the last 2 years, Genie Diapers has pulled all TV and print advertisements, which has led to loss of mindshare among customers.

Need marketing spend and market share trends

Need competitor marketing spend and market share trends

Need marketing spend by channel and market share trends

Need competitor marketing spend by channel and market share trends

> DISTRIBUTION HYPOTHESES: Due to a lack of a functioning e-commerce site, Genie Diapers is wholly dependent on retail stores, which leads to lower sales among millennials.

Need margins by channel over time

Need market share by channel

THE STRATEGY JOURNAL

step 16: COMPLETE THE FINANCIAL BENCHMARKING

You can approximate the size of the opportunity in two ways. First, from the financial analyses, you may find that the e-commerce market for diapers is worth $200M. Assuming Genie Diapers achieves the same market share in that channel as it does in other channels, 20%, the opportunity is worth $40M / annum.

The other way to find the size of the opportunity is via benchmarks. If all of Genie Diapers' competitors are spending $10M on marketing for roughly the same sales volume, and Genie Diapers is spending $20M, that means Genie Diapers has a $10M opportunity to lower marketing spend. Finding the size of the opportunity is important to understand if the problem is worth solving in the first place. It does not mean Genie Diapers will gain all the benefit. However, if the client and you, the consultant, believe obtaining even 30% ($3M) of the lowered marketing spend benefit is possible, you can decide if it is worth the effort. Most firms, especially smaller boutique consultants, are unlikely to have detailed benchmarks.

However, not having the benchmarks is not a reason to stop. You can interview competitors. Even without benchmarks, you can find opportunities in the financial analyses. A spike in costs and/or creeping costs are problems, even without knowing competitor metrics. The opportunities will rarely be hidden. Even if you skip some financial ratios, the same problem will show up in different areas, so you are likely to find it. Ignore the sections that are not relevant to you. You do not need lots of competitor data for benchmarks. Two competitors will provide enough insights.

#1 WHAT IS THE CONDITION OF THE BUSINESS?

#2 WHICH PARTS ARE RESPONSIBLE FOR THIS?

CASH **Genie Diapers Comp #1 #2**
Current ratio
Working capital

PROFITS GD Comp #1 #2
Return on sales:
Profit margin
Gross margin
Return on net assets
Return on equity

SOLVENCY GD Comp #1 #2
Debt equity ratio

INVESTMENTS GD Comp #1 #2
Price-earnings ratio
Earning per share

OVERALL GD Comp #1 #2
Costs breakdown

PRODUCT GD Comp #1 #2
Return on sales:
Profit margin
Gross margin
Sales
Volume
Pricing

REGION GD Comp #1 #2
Return on sales:
Profit margin
Gross margin
Sales
Volume
Pricing

#3 WHAT IS HAPPENING IN THE PROBLEM STATEMENT AREAS?

PRICING HYPOTHESIS GD Comp #1 #2
Price and market share trends
Competitor price and market share trends

PRODUCT HYPOTHESIS GD Comp #1 #2
Need product improvement rollout schedule and market share changes
Need competitor product improvement rollout schedule and market share changes

MARKETING HYPOTHESIS GD Comp #1 #2
Marketing spend and market share trends
Competitor marketing spend and market share trends
Marketing spend by channel and market share trends
Competitor marketing spend by channel and market share trends

DISTRIBUTION HYPOTHESIS GD Comp #1 #2
Margins by channel over time
Market share by channels

step 17: COMPLETE THE CASE STUDIES

Case studies are powerful tools to give the client both comfort about what is possible and a context for what to expect. You need not even do case studies of companies in the same sector. Companies of comparable size in other sectors case studied for a specific issue that is important to the client will be fine.

Larger consulting firms will have detailed case studies. However, that is not always an advantage. Case studies are an author's interpretation of an event. Therefore, when a larger firm presents stacks of case studies from previous studies, it rarely means the team using the case study will understand the issues presented, since the case study was written by an author who probably left the firm, or has not briefed the team on the nuances of his or her approach and/or findings. Those case studies become sound-bites that oversimplify a topic.

Boutique firms should focus on making the case study valuable. Focus on the *one* reason why something failed or succeeded. If a case-studied company did 12 things to make an initiative succeed, find that one critical thing done and understand what happened. That is more valuable than discussing 11 interesting items that have not been properly researched. In other words, don't focus on the volume of reasons. If you are just a one-person firm and you want to find out how Genie Diapers' competitors entered e-commerce, or similar companies entered e-commerce, simply interview university professors who have studied them. In other cases, you can find ex-employees and even current employees on LinkedIn. If you are upfront about your intentions and promise to anonymize the data, they will usually talk to you.

Keep each case study focused on a single narrow issue. You can do three case studies, but each must be specific to one issue. One can be about the problems a company faced transitioning to e-commerce. Another can be about costs, and the last can be about hiring. Avoid the urge to simply copy what you find via Google searches. You will not help the client. In the short term, the client may be satisfied with information from Google, but if the results are incorrect, your recommendations will eventually cause problems.

CASE STUDY OF NEW YORK TOILETRIES

NEW YORK TOILETRIES	WHAT ARE THE MOST IMPORTANT REASONS THIS FAILED/SUCCEEDED?
$1.2B revenue. $6.4B market cap. 10,000 employees. 23 brands. 25% sales from own digital store.	Rebates, incentives and shelf-space promotion costs kept going up with retailers. Cost of training, retaining, and managing the sales staff was creeping up. Competitors were taking away the best in-store shelf space and end-of-aisle promotions. In a competitive, low-unemployment market, these three costs were expected to rise. Management realized it had to find a new channel outside retail, since nothing was working to improve retail volumes in a cost-effective manner. The tipping point was the 3-year projections on the costs and sales through retail. The margins were small and expected to decline further.
ISSUES STUDIED How did New York Toiletries make the decision to launch their own digital store? What was the tipping point for the board of directors to make the investment?	
	IMPLEMENTATION LESSONS Start small, start immediately, and be willing to learn and adapt. Set up a dedicated team and get them going immediately. There was no perfect solution that could be bought off the shelf. They had to build it. Avoid excessive customization since it is expensive to build and maintain. Give up some features from off-the-shelf modules. Learning how to market online, manage direct consumer relationships was a skill they never had. They had to build B2C relationships. There is a financial payoff, but it takes longer than expected and costs more.
OUTCOME Distributes 50/50 of product via own store and Amazon. No longer dependent on Amazon. 50% of sales are digital.	
KEY LESSONS Did not separate e-commerce team. Product, R&D, marketing, etc., all made changes to support the e-commerce effort. E-commerce reported to CEO as a separate channel.	**STRATEGY LESSONS** Having multiple channels offers leverage to negotiate. E-commerce made them a B2C company and allowed them to learn directly from consumers, build relationships, and directly upsell to them. The support desk went from solving problems to helping customers understand what they wanted.

THE STRATEGY JOURNAL

step 18: PREPARE THE SLIDES FOR THE 2ND EXECUTIVE UPDATE

TOP 2 MESSAGES PER SECTION

BROAD FINANCIAL ANALYSES + BENCHMARKS	WHAT IS HAPPENING IN THE AREAS HYPOTHESIZED TO BE THE PROBLEM?	CASE STUDIES
PROFITS Overhead costs have risen 23% due to a tight labor market. Retail margins have dropped 12% in 12 months due to increased promotional competition.	**PRICING** Competitors have matched previous price decreases dollar-for-dollar, leading to fears about a price war. Historically, price decreases have not led to an increase in profits.	**CASE STUDY #1** Having multiple channels provides leverage to negotiate. E-commerce made them a B2C company and allowed them to learn directly from consumers, build relationships, and directly upsell to them. The support desk went from solving problems to helping customers understand what they wanted.
OVERALL The overall US business is showing a 3% decline in profits. Dense, fast-growing urban areas are showing a 12% decline and rural areas 7% growth.	**PRODUCT** 27% of all complaints received are about the lack of waterproof tape on diapers. 19% of all complaints received are about the limited carry pack options.	**CASE STUDY #2** Starting with Amazon is useful. Their demands for lower costs forces suppliers to bring their costs under control before setting up their own e-commerce channel. It is very difficult to beat Amazon on price.
PRODUCT Carry-pack diapers, popular in urban areas, are growing 23% YOY, and we are absent from this size segment. Consumers are willing to pay up to a 6% premium for waterproof diaper tape and will change brands for this feature.	**MARKETING** Only 3% of our ad spend is online, and we have no relationships with online bloggers. Marketing spending has grown 7% faster than volume growth in the last 5 years.	**CASE STUDY #3** Support centers that advise customers on products, planning their babies needs, etc., can charge a premium and result in larger basket sizes. Only works where there is direct access to the consumer.
REGION Profits in the Sand States have dropped 7% in the last year. Yet, they are projected to grow 5% YOY once the current sales expansion investments end in 4 months.	**DISTRIBUTION** Our e-commerce budget averages 45% under-expenditure for the last 4 years. 4 of the 10 largest wholesalers do not have dedicated sales reps, ~ 42% of all wholesale volume.	
CASH ON HAND / SOLVENCY / INVESTMENTS N/A		

WHAT HAPPENS NEXT

Keep refining each message. Expect it to take a few rounds of edits. Change the order of the messages to create a compelling overall story. Each message becomes the headline of a slide.

The body of the slide will be created from the financial analyses, benchmarking, and/or case study findings that support the headline. Use a mix of charts, tables, and quotes. However, keep the slides simple with just one exhibit per slide.

THE STRATEGY JOURNAL

step 19: THE 2ND EXECUTIVE UPDATE

SECTIONS IN THE UPDATE

WHERE WE ARE

Show 4 slides

1. Slide: Problem statement + tree.
2. Slide: Timeline.
3. Slide: Charter.
4. Slide: 3 most important messages you will deliver today. This is your executive summary.

REVIEW WHAT WE FOUND IN FOCUS INTERVIEWS

Show 2 slides

1. Most important finding #1
2. Most important finding #2

FINANCIAL ANALYSES

Show 4-6 slides

1. What are the problem areas you will investigate further?
2. Tell a story.

BENCHMARKS

Show 2-3 slides

1. What is the estimated range of benefits if the client was more in line with peers.
2. What will be tested further?

CASE STUDIES

1. 1 slide per case study.
2. What is the most important reason the initiatives profiled failed/succeed?
3. Only show 1 case study if necessary or create one slide summarizing all the insights.

ASK THE CLIENT TO AGREE TO A DECISION

Show 1 slide

1. Now that we know x and y are not causing the problem to as large a degree, do we agree to focus on z?

WHAT YOU WILL SEE NEXT

1. Calculated validated benefits range.
2. Quick wins list.
3. Options to fix the problem.

WHAT HAPPENS NEXT

Having finished the focus interviews, financial analyses, benchmarks, and case studies, you can now be certain of the accuracy of your early hypotheses. It is very unlikely you could have missed anything that can derail your logic. Only in the 3rd update will you present your analyses to test the hypotheses.

You also know the range of the potential benefits. If the maximum of the range is too small, it raises doubts about the value of the work. Knowing earlier that the benefits to the client may be too small gives the team enough time to find more benefits.

The financial analyses, benchmarks, and case studies are best presented as a single story rather than as separate sections. For example, if labor costs, as depicted in the financial analyses, are shown to be too high, follow this up with a slide of labor cost benchmarks and another on a labor cost case study. By creating this story, the client is more likely to both understand and act on the finding.

> Notice how late in the engagement we present our core analyses? It is never done upfront, and we have *not* yet presented it with 50% of the engagement completed. Yet, the client is seeing progress because there is significant progress made, and we are well on track.
>
> There are two validation steps before we present our analyses. This is the second and final validation step. The first validation step was the focus interviews. We have now completed validating our thinking.

THE STRATEGY JOURNAL

step 20: VALIDATE YOUR PRELIMINARY STORYBOARD

Your preliminary storyboard would have been created the weekend before the study commenced or, at the latest, within the first two days of the study (steps 4 and 5). It would have been reasonably accurate and served a vital role, a role it continues to serve since it is a document that continually changes. It is your roadmap. Yet, it will not be perfect, and you should always expect the focus interviews, financial analyses, benchmarking, and case studies (collectively known as the top-down analyses) to highlight additional areas for analysis or a new interpretation of a problem you have already identified.

As you completed each of the top-down analyses, you should have been going back to see if the problem statement, decision-tree, hypotheses, tests for hypotheses, and eventually, the storyboard needed to be updated. It is an iterative and ongoing process. This is the formal step to check if the necessary updates have been done. This will be the ideal time to make any remaining updates to your analyses and resulting storyboard. Unnecessary/incorrect analyses waste time and money and will hurt your credibility as an advisor.

I IDENTIFIED THE CORRECT PROBLEM AND ROOT CAUSE IN MY PRELIMINARY STORY BOARD TO BE...

Diaper profits are going down.

Margins are lower due to non-premium features like waterproof tape.

We have no presence in the higher-margin e-commerce market.

THE FOCUS INTERVIEW DATA CORROBORATING THESE PROBLEMS/ROOT CAUSE WITH RANKINGS AND QOUTES ARE...

Quotes from finance and sales teams, and retailers.

Focus interviews on data from manager of a competitor who launched products on Amazon.

THE FINANCIAL ANALYSES, BENCHMARKING AND CASE STUDY DATA CORROBORATING THESE PROBLEMS/ROOT CAUSE ARE...

Finance manager reports.

Sales breakdown by channel from the finance team.

Case Study 2 and their investments and returns on waterproof tape.

FIXING THE PROBLEMS ABOVE WILL CREATE SUFFICIENT BANKABLE VALUE TO THE CLIENT, RELATIVE TO MY FEES, AND THE ESTIMATED IMPLEMENTATION FEES AND EFFORT, BECAUSE...

Most of the changes require the client to outsource the e-commerce channel management, which typically lowers fees, and the volume is so large, it could increase the sales volume of their entire business by 20%.

I HAVE IDENTIFIED THE FOLLOWING NEW PROBLEMS THAT THE CLIENT SHOULD FIX...

Sales costs are significantly higher than competitors.

HINT! You will ALWAYS find additional problems. That is one reason why the focus interviews and financial analyses are so broad.

This is the work you sell-on to the client. It is more efficient to generate new work from an existing engagement than trying to build a relationship at a new client.

Even with an existing client, it is better to be discussing new work while completing an existing study. Once the study ends, it is always tougher to obtain meetings.

WITH THE OPTIONS OF CHANGING THE SCOPE OF MY CURRENT WORK OR TREATING THIS AS A POTENTIAL NEW STUDY, I HAVE...

Decided to treat this as a potential new study because the sales staff cover more than the Genie Diapers brand, so this is not a Genie Diapers problem.

In the final two weeks, I will develop an opportunity chart and benefits case about the potential value of launching a study to fix this problem.

I will discuss this with the client outside of the 4th update.

PREPARING FOR THE 3ʳᴰ CLIENT UPDATE

week 5 to 6
OF THE STUDY

THE STRATEGY JOURNAL

step 21: COMPLETE THE ANALYSES

After two updates and 4 weeks of validating your initial thinking—focus interviews and financial analyses, case studies, and benchmarks—we now will complete the analyses. By completing the analyses we test the hypotheses. And if the tests show our hypotheses to be true, we have partially completed the study. We thereafter need to offer 2-3 options to fix the problem and calculate the net benefits of implementing the recommended option.

You should have started this in Week 2, but now is the final chance to go out and collect data to populate the exhibits below and see the results. Your headlines and numbers will certainly change (in grey underlined below) a little since the preliminary storyboard was an educated guess of what you expected to see if you did the test. Even with the correct numbers, the message should be roughly the same. Now that you have completed the test, determine if the overall story remains the same, even if the numbers change a little.

If you have methodically followed this approach, you should not see major changes. Your story would be valid, but now you have real data to back it up. Feel free to change the order of the slides to improve the story.

1. COLLECT DATA
X-axis
Y-axis
Check with client that the data is appropriate.
Clean data.
Adjust time periods.
Adjust for seasonality.
Adjust for industry changes.

2. POPULATE EXHIBIT
Insert real data in exhibit.
Isolate differences from exhibit with assumed data.
Note assumptions leading to differences.

3. KEY INSIGHT
What is the key message from this slide?
Is the original headline valid?
If valid, must it be updated?
If not valid, is the overall storyboard valid?

4. UPDATE HEADLINE
Will the slide be used?
If so, keep in storyboard.
If not, move to appendices.

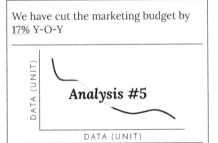

We have cut the marketing budget by 17% Y-O-Y

Analysis #5

analysis for **marketing**

Which has led to a 12% drop in customer mindshare in the same period

Analysis #6

analysis for **marketing**

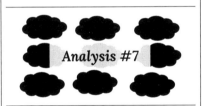

Yet, we still have financial reserves and margins 11% higher than competitors.

Analysis #7

analysis for **pricing**

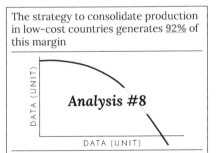

The strategy to consolidate production in low-cost countries generates 92% of this margin

Analysis #8

analysis for **pricing**

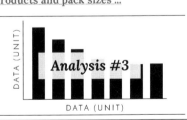

And this is needed to introduce new products and pack sizes ...

Analysis #3

analysis for **product**

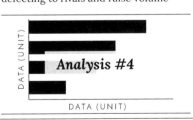

... which will lead to fewer customers defecting to rivals and raise volume

Analysis #4

analysis for **product**

A simultaneous investment in major online platforms offers direct access to the largest consumer segment

Analysis #1

analysis for **distribution**

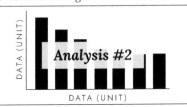

Assuming our share remains the same, we can raise volume 27% via e-commerce targeted to millennials

Analysis #2

analysis for **distribution**

THE STRATEGY JOURNAL

step 22: DOCUMENT OPPORTUNITIES TO THE CLIENT AS YOU FIND THEM

As you progress through the study, from weeks 1 to 6, you will find opportunities to fix the problem. For example, on the first Friday in Week 1 during a focus interview you may be told:

"By entering the e-commerce channel, Amazon will allow us to store our diapers in their warehouses."
Payal Mehra, Pricing Manager – Genie Diapers

You, therefore, realize there are 4 benefits to Genie Diapers:

1. Reduced warehouse leasing and labor costs.
2. Lower insurance bill due to less space to insure and less risky commercial warehouses to insure.
3. Avoided shipping costs since Amazon will pick up directly from the factory.
4. Less incentives paid to retailers/wholesalers since those channels lose their negotiating leverage.

Write out each opportunity in a separate document using the template below. To the client, the opportunities are the most important things. A strategy without clear opportunities to generate benefits will rarely work.

You will have a folder of these opportunities. As you get into weeks 5 and 6, the team must focus on adding numbers to these opportunities. This is discussed on the next page (step 23). Complete the next page only for opportunities that you intend to implement as part of the preferred option. An interesting and valid opportunity that is not part of the recommended option and, therefore, not a part of the proposed implementation should not be completed on the next page. You can keep these opportunities for a separate discussion for another possible study. They may be very valuable, just not helpful in solving this problem.

DESCRIPTION OF OPPORTUNITY

Opportunity:	Reduced warehouse and labor costs.	Created by:	Sanjeev Singh

What is not working/could be improved?	Describe the opportunity?	What must we change?
	Storage of finished goods inventory prior to B2C shipping.	Using Amazon to store diapers, reduces the need to build additional warehouses for diapers.

How do we know it is not working?	How is the process *currently* measured?		How good/bad is it today?	
	Measure 1 /KPI	Warehouse capacity utilization. →	Quantify	92%
	Measure 2 /KPI	Shipping cost as percentage of sales. →	Quantify	12%

If I change x, y, and z, the opportunity can be captured by the client.	x = Allow Amazon to sell diapers for Genie Diapers. y = Allow Amazon to lower prices/margin so they can push sufficient volume. z = Once volume passes threshold of 5% current volume, Amazon will take over warehousing.

How good could/should the process be? (Lead: How will we know we will eventually hit our target? Lag: How do we know it worked?)	How *could/should* we measure success for this opportunity?		Targets:	High Confidence	→	Stretch
	Lead/Lag KPI Measure 1	Purchases due to customers buying on Amazon after finding our product in search allows to reduce ad spend. →	Quantify	5% lower ad spend.	→	30%
	Lead/Lag KPI Measure 2	Priced marginally lower than retail. →	Quantify	2% below retail price.	→	3%
	Lead/Lag KPI Measure 1	Warehousing costs avoided. →	Quantify	5%	→	7%

Opportunity Sheet Developed With:

Name:	Gina Smith	Dept./Title:	Finance / Manager	Completed:	23 June 20____
Name:	Fei Zhou	Dept./Title:	Property / Analyst	Completed:	23 June 20____

THE STRATEGY JOURNAL

step 23: AGREE OPPORTUNITY CALCULATIONS, WITH EMPLOYEES, SO THEY BECOME BENEFITS

Take all opportunity sheets from step 22 and prioritize them by the size of the benefit and the probability of implementation. Sheets with the largest benefit with the highest probability of implementation should go to the top. Take this list and start with the first opportunity, the one at the top. Let's assume this is the opportunity we decide goes at the top: **1. Reduced warehouse and labor costs**.

We must find respected Genie Diaper employees with knowledge of the warehouse costs, real estate planning, utilization rates, and labor costs to test our benefit. We must gain their agreement that warehousing leasing requirements will decline, and labor costs will go down, and they need to accept the range of the savings we calculate. This means we must take the time to complete the calculations and obtain their approval. If they do not agree with your logic and range of savings, the opportunity remains an opportunity and cannot be presented as a benefit.

Let's assume they agree to this benefit but make some changes. Since the e-commerce channel will lead to an increase in the volume of diapers sold, **additional diaper volumes will be managed by Amazon, and there will not be a net reduction in the number of** existing warehouses and labor costs. Therefore, the employees classify the benefit as capital and labor costs that are avoided rather than reduced. Since Amazon will manage only the new volume once it reaches a certain threshold, they believe there will be a short-term spike in existing warehouse labor costs. The benefits calculation for this opportunity must reflect a short-term increase in costs.

Clients do not want to hear vague plans. They want to know exactly what to do and what are the individual initiatives to pursue, which together add up to the overall benefit from the new strategy. This approach naturally creates an implementation road map, accelerates implementation, and makes implementation easier. Benefits that can be implemented quickly with little effort are called quick wins. Clients want to see them, so you should separate quick win opportunity and benefit sheets. As you add up the benefits, estimate the cost to the client to implement them, the time for the benefit to show up in the client's bank account, and the return on the investment. You should present one slide with this net benefit from all the opportunities you have validated with the client employees.

DESCRIPTION OF BENEFIT TO CLIENT

Opportunity:	Reduced warehouse and labor costs	Created by:	Sanjeev Singh

Where in the financial statements can we track the improvement from fixing this opportunity?

- Improving the KPIs can have one (or more) of seven main financial benefits:

  Tick as relevant:
  - ☐ Sell more product
  - ☐ Sell a greater proportion of high-margin products
  - ☐ Raise prices
  - ☐ Reduce a current cost
  - ☒ Avoid a future cost
  - ☒ Eliminate the need for or (growth of) some portion of an asset (eg. premises, plant and equipment, etc.)
  - ☒ Reduce / avoid capital provisions by avoiding / reducing a risk

- How big is the revenue/cost/asset/risk base that would be impacted? ~20% of all diaper sales

- Key assumptions in the analysis/other comments (attach calculations and sources). Amazon is a large enough distributor. Small price savings will be large enough to entice customers to purchase on Amazon. Genie Diapers will capture the same market share in digital. Retailers will likely not punish Genie Diapers for undercutting them on price.

- If the KPIs improved by x% and y%, how much would the benefit increase

High confidence target = x	%5, $20M	Stretch target = y	%8, $32M

- How quickly would the benefit be realised and what would it cost

Date (month/week)	W0	W1	W2	W3	W4	W5	W6	W7	W8	W9	W10	W11	W12
Benefit % realised	0	0	0	0	0	5%	10%	20%	20%	20%	20%	5%	-
Investment to realise	0	0	0	$0.3M	$0.3M	0	0	0	0	0	0	0	0

- What are the top 3 risks to not realizing the benefits? 1) Hire new warehouse staff and sales volume does not increase. 2) Competitors lower prices. 3) Amazon changes its terms which will make it not attractive for Genie Diapers to use Amazon warehouse option or even to sell on Amazon.

Financial Logic Developed With:

Name:	Gina Smith	Dept./Title:	Finance / Manager	Completed:	30 June 20____
Name:	Fei Zhou	Dept./Title:	Property / Analyst	Completed:	30 June 20____

THE STRATEGY JOURNAL

step 24: THE 3ʳᴰ EXECUTIVE UPDATE

SECTIONS IN THE UPDATE

WHERE WE ARE
Show 4 slides
1. Slide: Problem statement + tree.
2. Slide: Timeline.
3. Slide: Charter.
4. Slide: 3 most important messages you will deliver today. This is the executive summary.

REVIEW WHAT WE FOUND IN OUR ANALYSES
Show the main storyboard: 5 – 10 slides
1. Tight and focused story.

VALIDATING THE BENEFITS CASE
Show 4-6 slides
1. Slide: All benefits on matrix: size vs. ease of implementation.
2. Slide: Net benefit of all benefits minus investment costs.
3. Slides on 3 top benefits.
4. List of quick wins + net benefits.

OPTIONS FOR CLIENT
Show 4 slides
1. Slide: All options.
2. Slide: Trade-offs option 1.
3. Slide: Trade-offs option 2.
4. Slide: Trade-offs option 3.
5. Showing each option on a separate slide is optional.

ASK THE CLIENT TO AGREE TO A DECISION
Show 1 slide
1. Do we agree that Option 3 is the option we will analyze going forward?

INITIAL IMPLEMENTATION PLAN
1. Slide: Quick wins timeline.
2. Slide: Planning implementation.

WHAT YOU WILL SEE NEXT
1. Updated benefits case with selected option.
2. Revised implementation plan.
3. Revised quick wins and initial results.

WHAT HAPPENS NEXT

The 3ʳᵈ update is your final major update. You present your analysis verifying the problem and what you believe are the options to fix the problem. There is always more than one path to fixing the problem. Each path is an option with different risks, returns and trade-offs. Most consulting firms flip this approach around and present this analysis very early with stacks of charts to have a thud factor, one they feel is impactful. They use this part to generate credibility. This is a very stressful approach because it forces consultants to complete unnecessary analyses in unrealistic timelines, with questionable findings. You should, therefore, present this analysis later by leveraging the credibility earned from the two earlier updates.

So, what is the purpose of the 4ᵗʰ update to follow?

The 8 working days before the 4ᵗʰ update is a time to meet as many key executives as possible to ensure they understand the benefits case for implementing the recommendations. Therefore, the 4ᵗʰ update is one in which the client is effectively agreeing to the smaller first implementation phase.

Implementation for the quick wins should begin **before** the 4ᵗʰ update. In the next 8 days between the 3ʳᵈ and 4ᵗʰ updates you want at least 1, but preferably 2, quick wins **implemented** so that you can present them in the 4ᵗʰ update. At least a few quick wins can be easily implemented without requiring senior approval, so this will be possible.

Presenting a quick win that has been implemented by employees with verified banked benefits creates momentum by moving the study from planning to reality. Most consultants struggle with this transition and wait for the implementation phase to be approved. This delays the process and often offers rival consulting firms an opportunity to compete for the work. By generating results from the quick wins, and banking some benefits, the client is more likely to start the implementation phase immediately to avoid losing momentum.

PREPARING
FOR THE
4ᵀᴴ CLIENT UPDATE

week 7 to 8

OF THE STUDY

THE STRATEGY JOURNAL

step 25: THE 4ᵀᴴ EXECUTIVE UPDATE

SECTIONS IN THE UPDATE

WHERE WE ARE
Show 3 slides
1. Slide: Problem statement + tree.
2. Slide: Timeline.
3. Slide: 3 most important messages you will deliver today. This is the executive summary.

WHAT WE PRESENTED PREVIOUSLY
Show 5 slides
1. 3 slides on the main analysis findings.
2. Options to fix problem.
3. Net benefits of all options from the 3rd update.

REFINED BENEFITS
Show 1 slide
1. Slide showing any updates to final benefit total number.
2. There will always be some updates.

BANKED QUICK WIN BENEFITS
Show 2 slides
1. Quick wins implemented and value created for client.
2. Quick wins that can be implemented in the next month if implementation is approved.

IMPLEMENTATION PLAN
Show 1 slide
1. Implementation plan.
2. How to not lose momentum on the implementation.
3. Always show phases.

ASK THE CLIENT TO AGREE TO A DECISION
Show 1 slide
1. Do you agree to extend the engagement by 1 month to implement x benefits with verified estimates of y$?

WHAT YOU WILL SEE NEXT
Show 1 slide
1. Update on net benefit from quick wins implementation.
2. Implementation scorecard.
3. Implementation plan.

WHAT HAPPENS NEXT

The engagement blends into the implementation phase. Even when clients want a complete stop to a study, implementation of the quick wins is usually permitted. Clients will need to, rightly, go through formal procurement processes to award a multimillion-dollar implementation phase, which will cause delays. A client is, however, usually able and willing to approve a 1-month extension to the current project, especially with a reduced team where the objectives and benefits of the 1-month extension are clear: implementing quick wins while the benefits are being validated by their own employees, who are enthusiastic about the work.

By implementing some of the quick wins, client employees start pushing for implementation because they see the banked benefits from the quick wins. Employees want to be part of something that works. It helps with their performance reviews and bonuses. It helps with their promotion prospects. Therefore, employees will ask for the implementation to continue if the quick wins start generating results.

Consequently, implementation stops being "*just another*" engagement the consultant is trying to sell. The implementation becomes something the company wants to do, pushed by employees. This allows the consultants to stay with the client, keep billing, and continue working on the implementation planning.

This method is different from the approach most consultants use of coming in cold and trying to create a mindset change, via change management, to build momentum for implementation. This forces consultants to try to sell the idea of implementation to the employees.

This is also a different model from consultants who offer to work for free to develop the initial business case, with the goal of gaining an edge in being awarded the large and stable implementation engagement. Working for free is generally a bad idea unless you have a clear strategy on how to move to billed work.

It is safer to build up a smaller implementation engagement into a larger engagement, instead of asking for the full implementation to start right at the beginning.

Like every update, asking for this extension will not be awkward because the contents have been pre-presented to all the client executives in the update meeting. They have had an opportunity to ask questions, understand the process, and signal their agreement. Therefore, the consultant already knows this has been approved before the 4th update meeting even begins.

WORK ON YOUR STUDY

Now it is time to work on your study and deliver measurable financial benefits to your client/employer. Your clients—or your colleagues for those applying these skills inside their corporate and/or start-up—should be materially better off than before you started working with them. Use this Journal daily on your study. Use it to plan your day, use it in meetings, since it contains all the material to manage the engagement, and use it to wrap up your day. It should be your companion throughout, and you will see an improvement in your work.

NOTES

THE STRATEGY JOURNAL

step a: BUILD A DECISION-TREE OF OPTIONS TO SOLVE THE PROBLEM

PROBLEM	DECISION TREE OF DIRECT DRIVERS	RANK OPTIONS

step b: DEVELOP YOUR HYPOTHESIS FOR EACH PRIORITIZED OPTION

HYPOTHESES

| #1 Option | #2 | #3 |
| Hypothesis | | |

| #4 | #5 | #6 |

| #7 | #8 | #9 |

| #10 | #11 | #12 |

THE STRATEGY JOURNAL

step c: WRITE OUT THE TEST FOR EACH HYPOTHESIS, INCLUDE X AND Y AXES FOR EACH GRAPH

ANALYSES

#1 Hypothesis	#2	#3
Test for hypothesis		

#4	#5	#6

#7	#8	#9

#10	#11	#12

THE STRATEGY JOURNAL

step d+e: WRITE THE MAIN FINDING FROM EACH TEST AND ARRANGE THE PRELIMINARY STORYBOARD

BUILDING YOUR STORYBOARD

Iteration #1 **Iteration #2** **Iteration #n**

My story of the analyses is compelling, factual, riveting and will encourage the client to act because…

a)

b)

c)

It is financially beneficial for the client to fix this problem because…

a)

b)

c)

THE STRATEGY JOURNAL

step f+g: COMPLETE YOUR CHARTER AND, IF NEEDED, ADAPT THE PROJECT LOGIC

Objectives	Key Activities	Deliverables
Scope		**Critical Success Factors**

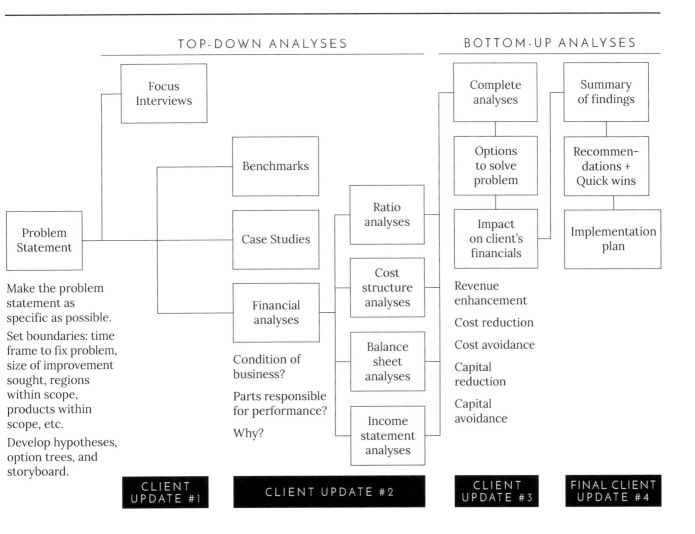

TOP-DOWN ANALYSES

BOTTOM-UP ANALYSES

Problem Statement

Make the problem statement as specific as possible.

Set boundaries: time frame to fix problem, size of improvement sought, regions within scope, products within scope, etc.

Develop hypotheses, option trees, and storyboard.

- Focus Interviews
- Benchmarks
- Case Studies
- Financial analyses
  - Condition of business?
  - Parts responsible for performance?
  - Why?
- Ratio analyses
- Cost structure analyses
- Balance sheet analyses
- Income statement analyses

- Complete analyses
- Options to solve problem
- Impact on client's financials

- Summary of findings
- Recommendations + Quick wins
- Implementation plan

Revenue enhancement
Cost reduction
Cost avoidance
Capital reduction
Capital avoidance

CLIENT UPDATE #1   CLIENT UPDATE #2   CLIENT UPDATE #3   FINAL CLIENT UPDATE #4

THE STRATEGY JOURNAL

step h: ADAPT YOUR TIMELINE & COMPLETE YOUR EXPECTATIONS EXCHANGE

WEEK 0 + 1	WEEK 2	WEEK 3	WEEK 4	WEEK 5	WEEK 6	WEEK 7	WEEK 8
	Update 1			**Update 2**		**Update 3**	**Update 4**
Charter ☐				Finish hypotheses testing ☐		Implement quick wins ☐	
Timelines ☐				Develop opportunities ☐		Bank benefits ☐	
Project logic ☐				Convert opportunities to benefits ☐		Finalize the size of the prize ☐	
Expectations exchange ☐				Validate the size of the prize ☐		Implementation plan ☐	
Hypotheses ☐	Financial analyses		☐	Identify quick wins ☐			
Storyboard ☐	Benchmarks		☐	Validate problems ☐			
Focus interview prep ☐	Case studies		☐	Options to address problems ☐			
	Range of the size of the prize		☐				
Knowledge capture planning ☐	Start testing hypotheses		☐				

EXPECTATIONS EXCHANGE

....

....

....

....

....

....

....

....

....

....

....

....

....

....

....

....

....

PREPARING
FOR THE
1ˢᵀ CLIENT UPDATE

week 1

OF THE STUDY

THE STRATEGY JOURNAL

NOTES

THE STRATEGY JOURNAL

step i: PREPARE YOUR FOCUS INTERVIEW QUESTIONS: SOLE CONTENT FOR THE 1ST EXECUTIVE UPDATE

Ask the questions in the white blocks, while making changes to customize them to your specific study and client. Keep them broad, so they allow you to find problems you may not be aware of. They help you see the blind spot(s) in your thinking. Go back to your hypotheses and look at the tests you will run. If there are any tests that can be completed with data from the focus interviews, add those questions in the blank blocks.

COMPANY PERFORMANCE

Is the company profitable?

Is the company as profitable as it could be?

What has been the general trend for revenue, costs and profits?

Why do you believe it has performed the way it has?

What should be the top 5 priorities to improve performance?

How would you rank these 5 priorities?

Do you believe costs are under control? Why?

MARKET STRUCTURE

What are the major product segments?

What are the needs for each segment?

How well are we meeting the needs? Rank us out of 5 alongside competitors.

Are there any segments not being served well?

Can those segments with unmet needs ever be served?

Is the company serving its segments to the best of its ability?

What successes and failures have you had, and what do you ascribe these to?

CUSTOMERS

Who are the primary customers of the business?

What are their top 5 needs?

Can you rank these 5 needs?

Are they served to the best of the company's ability?

What successes and/or failures have we had serving customers?

Are there customers with unmet needs we are not serving?

COMPETITORS

Who are our direct and indirect competitors?

Can you rank them based on their success level?

If we added our company to the ranking, where would it go?

Are competitors doing anything better/worse than you to serve customers?

Do our competitors have the same business model?

What new innovations have competitors released in the last 3 years?

How have we responded to these innovations?

Have we responded to the best of our ability?

What more could we do? Priorities?

CULTURE

What words would you use to describe the culture at the company?

Can you rank that list in order of most applicable to least applicable?

Has the culture improved or deteriorated?

Why did you provide the answer above?

Are there opportunities to improve the culture?

What changes would you like to see if you could introduce them?

INVESTMENTS

What investments are being made for the long-term?

Do you believe these are the correct investments?

Do you believe the investments are sufficient?

What do you think should be the priorities?

How would you rank these priorities?

THE STRATEGY JOURNAL

Date _____ / _____ / _____   Week #1

START YOUR DAY

To complete my critical path work, today people owe me…

To complete my critical path work, today I owe people…

END YOUR DAY

The potential opportunities I have identified for the benefits case are…

DELIGHTING MY CLIENT

I realize it is not my right to serve this client and will demonstrate to the client that I understand it is a privilege to serve them today by…

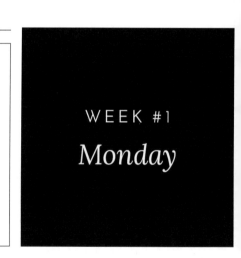

WEEK #1

Monday

WEEK 0 + 1	WEEK 2	WEEK 3	WEEK 4	WEEK 5	WEEK 6	WEEK 7	WEEK 8
	Update 1			Update 2		Update 3	Update 4
Charter ☐				Finish hypotheses testing ☐			
Timelines ☐				Develop opportunities ☐		Implement quick wins ☐	
Project logic ☐				Convert opportunities to benefits ☐		Bank benefits ☐	
Expectations exchange ☐				Validate the size of the prize ☐		Finalize the size of the prize ☐	
Hypotheses ☐	Financial analyses ☐			Identify quick wins ☐		Implementation plan ☐	
Storyboard ☐	Benchmarks ☐			Validate problems ☐			
Focus interview prep ☐	Case studies ☐			Options to address problems ☐			
	Range of the size of the prize ☐						
Knowledge capture planning ☐	Start testing hypotheses ☐						

THE STRATEGY JOURNAL

Week #1

NOTES

WEEK #1

Monday

THE STRATEGY JOURNAL

Date _____ / _____ / _____

Week #1

START YOUR DAY

To complete my critical path work, today people owe me…

To complete my critical path work, today I owe people…

END YOUR DAY

The potential opportunities I have identified for the benefits case are…

DELIGHTING MY CLIENT

I realize it is not my right to serve this client and will demonstrate to the client that I understand it is a privilege to serve them today by…

WEEK #1

Tuesday

WEEK 0 + 1	WEEK 2	WEEK 3	WEEK 4	WEEK 5	WEEK 6	WEEK 7	WEEK 8
	Update 1			Update 2		Update 3	Update 4
Charter ☐				Finish hypotheses testing ☐			
Timelines ☐				Develop opportunities ☐		Implement quick wins ☐	
Project logic ☐				Convert opportunities to benefits ☐		Bank benefits ☐	
Expectations exchange ☐				Validate the size of the prize ☐		Finalize the size of the prize ☐	
Hypotheses ☐	Financial analyses ☐			Identify quick wins ☐		Implementation plan ☐	
Storyboard ☐	Benchmarks ☐			Validate problems ☐			
Focus interview prep ☐	Case studies ☐			Options to address problems ☐			
	Range of the size of the prize ☐						
Knowledge capture planning ☐	Start testing hypotheses ☐						

RESERVE YOUR SPOT. FREE EX-MCK PARTNER EPISODES AT FIRMSCONSULTING.COM/PROMO

THE STRATEGY JOURNAL

Week #1

NOTES

WEEK #1
Tuesday

THE STRATEGY JOURNAL

Date _____ / _____ / _____   **Week #1**

START YOUR DAY

| To complete my critical path work, today people owe me… | To complete my critical path work, today I owe people… |

END YOUR DAY

The potential opportunities I have identified for the benefits case are…

DELIGHTING MY CLIENT

I realize it is not my right to serve this client and will demonstrate to the client that I understand it is a privilege to serve them today by…

WEEK #1

Wednesday

WEEK 0 + 1	WEEK 2	WEEK 3	WEEK 4	WEEK 5	WEEK 6	WEEK 7	WEEK 8
	Update 1			Update 2		Update 3	Update 4
Charter ☐				Finish hypotheses testing ☐			
Timelines ☐				Develop opportunities ☐		Implement quick wins ☐	
Project logic ☐				Convert opportunities to benefits ☐		Bank benefits ☐	
Expectations exchange ☐				Validate the size of the prize ☐		Finalize the size of the prize ☐	
Hypotheses ☐	Financial analyses ☐			Identify quick wins ☐		Implementation plan ☐	
Storyboard ☐	Benchmarks ☐			Validate problems ☐			
Focus interview prep ☐	Case studies ☐			Options to address problems ☐			
	Range of the size of the prize ☐						
Knowledge capture planning ☐	Start testing hypotheses ☐						

78   RESERVE YOUR SPOT. FREE EX-MCK PARTNER EPISODES AT FIRMSCONSULTING.COM/PROMO

THE STRATEGY JOURNAL

Week #1

NOTES

WEEK #1
Wednesday

THE STRATEGY JOURNAL

Date _____ / _____ / _____

Week #1

START YOUR DAY

To complete my critical path work, today people owe me...

To complete my critical path work, today I owe people...

END YOUR DAY

The potential opportunities I have identified for the benefits case are...

DELIGHTING MY CLIENT

I realize it is not my right to serve this client and will demonstrate to the client that I understand it is a privilege to serve them today by...

WEEK #1
Thursday

WEEK 0 + 1	WEEK 2	WEEK 3	WEEK 4	WEEK 5	WEEK 6	WEEK 7	WEEK 8
	Update 1			Update 2		Update 3	Update 4
Charter ☐				Finish hypotheses testing ☐			
Timelines ☐				Develop opportunities ☐		Implement quick wins ☐	
Project logic ☐				Convert opportunities to benefits ☐		Bank benefits ☐	
Expectations exchange ☐				Validate the size of the prize ☐		Finalize the size of the prize ☐	
				Identify quick wins ☐		Implementation plan ☐	
Hypotheses ☐	Financial analyses			Validate problems ☐			
Storyboard ☐	Benchmarks			Options to address problems ☐			
Focus interview prep ☐	Case studies						
	Range of the size of the prize						
Knowledge capture planning ☐	Start testing hypotheses						

THE STRATEGY JOURNAL

Week #1

NOTES

WEEK #1
Thursday

THE STRATEGY JOURNAL

step j: PREPARE THE SLIDES FOR THE 1ST EXECUTIVE UPDATE

FOCUS INTERVIEW

Top 2 messages per focus interview section

SECTIONS IN THE UPDATE

FOCUS INTERVIEW		SECTIONS IN THE UPDATE
COMPANY PERFORMANCE	SECTION TESTING SPECIFIC HYPOTHESES	**WHERE WE ARE** Show 4 slides 1. Slide: Problem statement + tree. 2. Slide: Timeline. 3. Slide: Charter. 4. Slide: 3 most important messages you will deliver today. This is your executive summary.
MARKET STRUCTURE	SECTION TESTING SPECIFIC HYPOTHESES	**WHAT WE FOUND IN FOCUS INTERVIEWS: BROAD SECTION** Show 6-10 slides 1. Tell a story. 2. Don't cover every section unless it is part of the story.
CUSTOMERS	SECTION TESTING SPECIFIC HYPOTHESES	**WHAT WE FOUND IN FOCUS INTERVIEWS: HYPOTHESES TESTED** Show 4-6 slides 1. Tell a story. 2. Don't cover every section unless it is part of the story. 3. Raise issues that will be addressed in future updates.
COMPETITORS	SECTION TESTING SPECIFIC HYPOTHESES	**ASK THE CLIENT TO AGREE TO A DECISION** Show 1 slide 1. Now that we know x and y are not causing the problem to as large a degree, do we agree to focus on z?
CULTURE	SECTION TESTING SPECIFIC HYPOTHESES	**WHAT YOU WILL SEE NEXT** Show 1 slide 1. The initial upper/lower benefit range. 2. Financial analyses. 3. Benchmarks. 4. Case studies.
INVESTMENTS	SECTION TESTING SPECIFIC HYPOTHESES	

NOTES

THE STRATEGY JOURNAL

Date _____ / _____ / _____   **Week #1**

START YOUR DAY

| To complete my critical path work, today people owe me... | To complete my critical path work, today I owe people... |

END YOUR DAY

The potential opportunities I have identified for the benefits case are...

PRE-PRESENTING

I will ensure there are no surprises for the client and that the update meeting leads to a decision by pre-presenting the final draft update 1 slides to the client today by meeting...

WEEK #1

Friday

WEEK 0 + 1	WEEK 2	WEEK 3	WEEK 4	WEEK 5	WEEK 6	WEEK 7	WEEK 8
	Update 1			**Update 2**		**Update 3**	**Update 4**
Charter ☐				Finish hypotheses testing ☐			
Timelines ☐				Develop opportunities ☐		Implement quick wins ☐	
Project logic ☐				Convert opportunities to benefits ☐		Bank benefits ☐	
Expectations exchange ☐				Validate the size of the prize ☐		Finalize the size of the prize ☐	
Hypotheses ☐	Financial analyses ☐			Identify quick wins ☐		Implementation plan ☐	
Storyboard ☐	Benchmarks ☐			Validate problems ☐			
Focus interview prep ☐	Case studies ☐			Options to address problems ☐			
	Range of the size of the prize ☐						
Knowledge capture planning ☐	Start testing hypotheses ☐						

THE STRATEGY JOURNAL

Week #1

NOTES

WEEK #1

Friday

THE STRATEGY JOURNAL

step k: HOLD YOUR WEEKLY TEAM UPDATE

OBJECTIVE	SCHEDULE	TEMPERATURE LAST WEEK	TEMPERATURE THIS WEEK

Consultant:

Client:

Sponsor:

Champion:

Client Team Member:

ACCOMPLISHMENTS

KEY ISSUES

KEY NEXT STEPS....FROM TODAY

WHAT　　　　WHO　　WHEN

IMPLEMENTATION ISSUES

KEY NEXT STEPS....FROM PREVIOUS MEETING

WHAT　　　　WHO　　WHEN

| Concern | Normal | Positive |

COMPLETING THE FINANCIAL ANALYSES AND START TESTING HYPOTHESES

week 2
OF THE STUDY

THE STRATEGY JOURNAL

Date _____ / _____ / _____   Week #2

START YOUR DAY

To complete my critical path work, today people owe me...

To complete my critical path work, today I owe people...

END YOUR DAY

The potential opportunities I have identified for the benefits case are...

DELIGHTING MY CLIENT

I realize it is not my right to serve this client and will demonstrate to the client that I understand it is a privilege to serve them today by...

WEEK #2

Monday

WEEK 0-1	WEEK 2	WEEK 3	WEEK 4	WEEK 5	WEEK 6	WEEK 7	WEEK 8
	Update 1			Update 2		Update 3	Update 4
Charter ☐				Finish hypotheses testing ☐		Implement quick wins ☐	
Timelines ☐				Develop opportunities ☐		Bank benefits ☐	
Project logic ☐				Convert opportunities to benefits ☐		Finalize the size of the prize ☐	
Expectations exchange ☐				Validate the size of the prize ☐		Implementation plan ☐	
Hypotheses ☐	Financial analyses ☐			Identify quick wins ☐			
Storyboard ☐	Benchmarks ☐			Validate problems ☐			
Focus interview prep ☐	Case studies ☐			Options to address problems ☐			
	Range of the size of the prize ☐						
Knowledge capture planning ☐	Start testing hypotheses ☐						

88 RESERVE YOUR SPOT. FREE EX-MCK PARTNER EPISODES AT FIRMSCONSULTING.COM/PROMO

THE STRATEGY JOURNAL

Week #2

NOTES

WEEK #2

Monday

THE STRATEGY JOURNAL

step 1: ACT ON THE NEXT STEPS FROM THE 1ST CLIENT UPDATE MEETING

SECTIONS IN THE UPDATE

WHERE WE ARE
Show 4 slides
1. Slide: Problem statement + tree.
2. Slide: Timeline.
3. Slide: Charter.
4. Slide: 3 most important messages you will deliver today.

WHAT WE FOUND IN FOCUS INTERVIEWS: BROAD SECTION
Show 6-10 slides
1. Tell a story.
2. Don't cover every section unless it is part of the story.

WHAT WE FOUND IN FOCUS INTERVIEWS: HYPOTHESES TESTED
Show 4-6 slides
1. Tell a story.
2. Don't cover every section unless it is part of the story.
3. Raise issues that will be addressed in future updates.

ASK THE CLIENT TO AGREE TO A DECISION
Show 1 slide
1. Now that we know x and y are not causing the problem to as large a degree, do we agree to focus on z?

WHAT YOU WILL SEE NEXT
Show 1 slide
1. The initial upper/lower benefit range.
2. Financial analyses.
3. Benchmarks.
4. Case studies.

KEY NEXT STEPS…. FROM 1ST CLIENT UPDATE MEETING

WHAT	WHO	WHEN

NOTES

THE STRATEGY JOURNAL

Date _____ / _____ / _____   **Week #2**

START YOUR DAY

| To complete my critical path work, today people owe me... | To complete my critical path work, today I owe people... |

END YOUR DAY

The potential opportunities I have identified for the benefits case are...

DELIGHTING MY CLIENT

I realize it is not my right to serve this client and will demonstrate to the client that I understand it is a privilege to serve them today by...

WEEK #2

Tuesday

WEEK 0 + 1	WEEK 2	WEEK 3	WEEK 4	WEEK 5	WEEK 6	WEEK 7	WEEK 8
	Update 1			**Update 2**		**Update 3**	**Update 4**
Charter ☐				Finish hypotheses testing ☐		Implement quick wins ☐	
Timelines ☐				Develop opportunities ☐		Bank benefits ☐	
Project logic ☐				Convert opportunities to benefits ☐		Finalize the size of the prize ☐	
Expectations exchange ☐				Validate the size of the prize ☐		Implementation plan ☐	
Hypotheses ☐	Financial analyses ☐			Identify quick wins ☐			
Storyboard ☐	Benchmarks ☐			Validate problems ☐			
Focus interview prep ☐	Case studies ☐			Options to address problems ☐			
	Range of the size of the prize ☐						
Knowledge capture planning ☐	Start testing hypotheses ☐						

THE STRATEGY JOURNAL

Week #2

NOTES

WEEK #2
Tuesday

THE STRATEGY JOURNAL

Date _____ / _____ / _____

Week #2

START YOUR DAY

To complete my critical path work, today people owe me...

To complete my critical path work, today I owe people...

END YOUR DAY

The potential opportunities I have identified for the benefits case are...

DELIGHTING MY CLIENT

I realize it is not my right to serve this client and will demonstrate to the client that I understand it is a privilege to serve them today by...

WEEK #2

Wednesday

WEEK 0 – 1	WEEK 2	WEEK 3	WEEK 4	WEEK 5	WEEK 6	WEEK 7	WEEK 8
	Update 1			Update 2		Update 3	Update 4
Charter ☐				Finish hypotheses testing ☐		Implement quick wins ☐	
Timelines ☐				Develop opportunities ☐		Bank benefits ☐	
Project logic ☐				Convert opportunities to benefits ☐		Finalize the size of the prize ☐	
Expectations exchange ☐				Validate the size of the prize ☐		Implementation plan ☐	
Hypotheses ☐	Financial analyses ☐			Identify quick wins ☐			
Storyboard ☐	Benchmarks ☐			Validate problems ☐			
Focus interview prep ☐	Case studies ☐			Options to address problems ☐			
	Range of the size of the prize ☐						
Knowledge capture planning ☐	Start testing hypotheses ☐						

94   RESERVE YOUR SPOT. FREE EX-MCK PARTNER EPISODES AT FIRMSCONSULTING.COM/PROMO

Week #2

NOTES

WEEK #2
Wednesday

THE STRATEGY JOURNAL

Date _____ / _____ / _____

Week #2

START YOUR DAY

To complete my critical path work, today people owe me…

To complete my critical path work, today I owe people…

END YOUR DAY

The potential opportunities I have identified for the benefits case are…

DELIGHTING MY CLIENT

I realize it is not my right to serve this client and will demonstrate to the client that I understand it is a privilege to serve them today by…

WEEK #2

Thursday

WEEK 0 + 1	WEEK 2	WEEK 3	WEEK 4	WEEK 5	WEEK 6	WEEK 7	WEEK 8
	Update 1			**Update 2**		**Update 3**	**Update 4**
Charter ☐				Finish hypotheses testing ☐		Implement quick wins ☐	
Timelines ☐				Develop opportunities ☐		Bank benefits ☐	
Project logic ☐				Convert opportunities to benefits ☐		Finalize the size of the prize ☐	
Expectations exchange ☐				Validate the size of the prize ☐		Implementation plan ☐	
Hypotheses ☐	Financial analyses ☐			Identify quick wins ☐			
Storyboard ☐	Benchmarks ☐			Validate problems ☐			
Focus interview prep ☐	Case studies ☐			Options to address problems ☐			
	Range of the size of the prize ☐						
Knowledge capture planning ☐	Start testing hypotheses ☐						

THE STRATEGY JOURNAL

Week #2

NOTES

WEEK #2
Thursday

THE STRATEGY JOURNAL

Date _____ / _____ / _____   Week #2

START YOUR DAY

| To complete my critical path work, today people owe me… | To complete my critical path work, today I owe people… |

END YOUR DAY

The potential opportunities I have identified for the benefits case are…

DELIGHTING MY CLIENT

I realize it is not my right to serve this client and will demonstrate to the client that I understand it is a privilege to serve them today by…

WEEK #2
Friday

WEEK 0+1	WEEK 2	WEEK 3	WEEK 4	WEEK 5	WEEK 6	WEEK 7	WEEK 8
	Update 1			**Update 2**		**Update 3**	**Update 4**
Charter ☐				Finish hypotheses testing ☐			
Timelines ☐				Develop opportunities ☐			
Project logic ☐				Convert opportunities to benefits ☐			
Expectations exchange ☐				Validate the size of the prize ☐			
Hypotheses ☐	Financial analyses ☐			Identify quick wins ☐			
Storyboard ☐	Benchmarks ☐			Validate problems ☐			
Focus interview prep ☐	Case studies ☐			Options to address problems ☐			
	Range of the size of the prize ☐						
Knowledge capture planning ☐	Start testing hypotheses ☐						

THE STRATEGY JOURNAL

Week #2

NOTES

WEEK #2

Friday

THE STRATEGY JOURNAL

step m: COMPLETE THE FINANCIAL ANALYSES

#1 WHAT IS THE CONDITION OF THE BUSINESS?

PROFITS
Return on sales:
Profit margin
Gross margin
Return on net assets
Return on equity

CASH
Current ratio
Working capital

SOLVENCY
Debt equity ratio

INVESTMENTS
Price-earnings ratio
Earning per share

#2 WHICH PARTS ARE RESPONSIBLE FOR THIS?

OVERALL
Costs breakdown

PRODUCT
Return on sales:
Profit margin
Gross margin
Sales
Volume
Pricing

REGION
Return on sales:
Profit margin
Gross margin
Sales
Volume
Pricing

#3 WHAT IS HAPPENING IN THE PROBLEM STATEMENT AREAS?

THE STRATEGY JOURNAL

step n: HOLD YOUR WEEKLY TEAM UPDATE

OBJECTIVE	SCHEDULE	TEMPERATURE LAST WEEK	TEMPERATURE THIS WEEK	
				Consultant: Client: Sponsor: Champion: Client Team Member:

ACCOMPLISHMENTS	KEY ISSUES	KEY NEXT STEPS….FROM TODAY WHAT WHO WHEN
	IMPLEMENTATION ISSUES	KEY NEXT STEPS….FROM PREVIOUS MEETING WHAT WHO WHEN

Concern   Normal   Positive

NOTES

COMPLETING THE CASE STUDIES AND BENCHMARKS

week 3

OF THE STUDY

THE STRATEGY JOURNAL

Date _____ / _____ / _____   Week #3

START YOUR DAY

To complete my critical path work, today people owe me...

To complete my critical path work, today I owe people...

END YOUR DAY

The potential opportunities I have identified for the benefits case are...

DELIGHTING MY CLIENT

I realize it is not my right to serve this client and will demonstrate to the client that I understand it is a privilege to serve them today by...

WEEK #3
Monday

WEEK 0+1	WEEK 2	WEEK 3	WEEK 4	WEEK 5	WEEK 6	WEEK 7	WEEK 8
	Update 1			Update 2		Update 3	Update 4
Charter ☐				Finish hypotheses testing ☐		Implement quick wins ☐	
Timelines ☐				Develop opportunities ☐		Bank benefits ☐	
Project logic ☐				Convert opportunities to benefits ☐		Finalize the size of the prize ☐	
Expectations exchange ☐				Validate the size of the prize ☐		Implementation plan ☐	
Hypotheses ☐	Financial analyses ☐			Identify quick wins ☐			
Storyboard ☐	Benchmarks ☐			Validate problems ☐			
Focus interview prep ☐	Case studies ☐			Options to address problems ☐			
	Range of the size of the prize ☐						
Knowledge capture planning ☐	Start testing hypotheses ☐						

RESERVE YOUR SPOT. FREE EX-MCK PARTNER EPISODES AT FIRMSCONSULTING.COM/PROMO

THE STRATEGY JOURNAL

Week #3

NOTES

WEEK #3

Monday

THE STRATEGY JOURNAL

Date _____ / _____ / _____

Week #3

START YOUR DAY

To complete my critical path work, today people owe me...

To complete my critical path work, today I owe people...

END YOUR DAY

The potential opportunities I have identified for the benefits case are...

DELIGHTING MY CLIENT

I realize it is not my right to serve this client and will demonstrate to the client that I understand it is a privilege to serve them today by...

WEEK #3

Tuesday

WEEK 0 + 1	WEEK 2	WEEK 3	WEEK 4	WEEK 5	WEEK 6	WEEK 7	WEEK 8
	Update 1			Update 2		Update 3	Update 4
Charter				Finish hypotheses testing ☐		Implement quick wins ☐	
Timelines				Develop opportunities ☐		Bank benefits ☐	
Project logic				Convert opportunities to benefits ☐		Finalize the size of the prize ☐	
Expectations exchange				Validate the size of the prize ☐		Implementation plan ☐	
Hypotheses		Financial analyses ☐		Identify quick wins ☐			
Storyboard		Benchmarks ☐		Validate problems ☐			
Focus interview prep		Case studies ☐		Options to address problems ☐			
		Range of the size of the prize ☐					
Knowledge capture planning		Start testing hypotheses ☐					

RESERVE YOUR SPOT. FREE EX-MCK PARTNER EPISODES AT FIRMSCONSULTING.COM/PROMO

Week #3

NOTES

**WEEK #3
Tuesday**

THE STRATEGY JOURNAL

Date _____ / _____ / _____   Week #3

START YOUR DAY

| To complete my critical path work, today people owe me... | To complete my critical path work, today I owe people... |

END YOUR DAY

The potential opportunities I have identified for the benefits case are...

DELIGHTING MY CLIENT

I realize it is not my right to serve this client and will demonstrate to the client that I understand it is a privilege to serve them today by...

WEEK #3

Wednesday

WEEK 0 + 1	WEEK 2	WEEK 3	WEEK 4	WEEK 5	WEEK 6	WEEK 7	WEEK 8
	Update 1			Update 2		Update 3	Update 4
Charter ☐				Finish hypotheses testing ☐		Implement quick wins ☐	
Timelines ☐				Develop opportunities ☐		Bank benefits ☐	
Project logic ☐				Convert opportunities to benefits ☐		Finalize the size of the prize ☐	
Expectations exchange ☐				Validate the size of the prize ☐		Implementation plan ☐	
Hypotheses ☐	Financial analyses ☐			Identify quick wins ☐			
Storyboard ☐	Benchmarks ☐			Validate problems ☐			
Focus interview prep ☐	Case studies ☐			Options to address problems ☐			
	Range of the size of the prize ☐						
Knowledge capture planning ☐	Start testing hypotheses ☐						

THE STRATEGY JOURNAL

Week #3

NOTES

WEEK #3
Wednesday

THE STRATEGY JOURNAL

Date _____ / _____ / _____

Week #3

START YOUR DAY

To complete my critical path work, today people owe me…

To complete my critical path work, today I owe people…

END YOUR DAY

The potential opportunities I have identified for the benefits case are…

DELIGHTING MY CLIENT

I realize it is not my right to serve this client and will demonstrate to the client that I understand it is a privilege to serve them today by…

WEEK #3

Thursday

WEEK 0 - 1	WEEK 2	WEEK 3	WEEK 4	WEEK 5	WEEK 6	WEEK 7	WEEK 8
	Update 1			Update 2		Update 3	Update 4
Charter ☐				Finish hypotheses testing ☐		Implement quick wins ☐	
Timelines ☐				Develop opportunities ☐		Bank benefits ☐	
Project logic ☐				Convert opportunities to benefits ☐		Finalize the size of the prize ☐	
Expectations exchange ☐				Validate the size of the prize ☐		Implementation plan ☐	
Hypotheses ☐		Financial analyses ☐		Identify quick wins ☐			
Storyboard ☐		Benchmarks ☐		Validate problems ☐			
Focus interview prep ☐		Case studies ☐		Options to address problems ☐			
		Range of the size of the prize ☐					
Knowledge capture planning ☐		Start testing hypotheses ☐					

THE STRATEGY JOURNAL

Week #3

NOTES

WEEK #3

Thursday

THE STRATEGY JOURNAL

Date _____ / _____ / _____   **Week #3**

START YOUR DAY

To complete my critical path work, today people owe me...

To complete my critical path work, today I owe people...

END YOUR DAY

The potential opportunities I have identified for the benefits case are...

DELIGHTING MY CLIENT

I realize it is not my right to serve this client and will demonstrate to the client that I understand it is a privilege to serve them today by...

WEEK #3

Friday

WEEK 0 + 1	WEEK 2	WEEK 3	WEEK 4	WEEK 5	WEEK 6	WEEK 7	WEEK 8
	Update 1			Update 2		Update 3	Update 4
Charter ☐				Finish hypotheses testing ☐		Implement quick wins ☐	
Timelines ☐				Develop opportunities ☐		Bank benefits ☐	
Project logic ☐				Convert opportunities to benefits ☐		Finalize the size of the prize ☐	
Expectations exchange ☐				Validate the size of the prize ☐		Implementation plan ☐	
Hypotheses ☐	Financial analyses ☐			Identify quick wins ☐			
Storyboard ☐	Benchmarks ☐			Validate problems ☐			
Focus interview prep ☐	Case studies ☐			Options to address problems ☐			
	Range of the size of the prize ☐						
Knowledge capture planning ☐	Start testing hypotheses ☐						

Week #3

NOTES

WEEK #3
Friday

THE STRATEGY JOURNAL

step 0: COMPLETE THE BENCHMARKING

WHAT IS THE SIZE OF THE OPPORTUNITY

#1 WHAT IS THE CONDITION OF THE BUSINESS?

PROFITS — Client Comp #1 #2
Return on sales:
Profit margin
Gross margin
Return on net assets
Return on equity

CASH — Client Comp #1 #2
Current ratio
Working capital

SOLVENCY — Client Comp #1 #2
Debt equity ratio

INVESTMENTS — Client Comp #1 #2
Price-earnings ratio
Earning per share

#2 WHICH PARTS ARE RESPONSIBLE FOR THIS?

OVERALL — Client Comp #1 #2
Costs breakdown

PRODUCT — Client Comp #1 #2
Return on sales:
Profit margin
Gross margin
Sales
Volume
Pricing

REGION — Client Comp #1 #2
Return on sales:
Profit margin
Gross margin
Sales
Volume
Pricing

#3 WHAT IS HAPPENING IN THE PROBLEM STATEMENT AREAS?

Client Comp #1 #2

Client Comp #1 #2

Client Comp #1 #2

Client Comp #1 #2

THE STRATEGY JOURNAL

step p: COMPLETE THE CASE STUDIES

CASE STUDY #1...

Name:	Business Case / Opportunity Lessons
Issues Studied	Implementation Lessons
Outcome	Strategy Lessons
Key Lessons	

NOTES

FREE EPISODE FROM BOOK'S COMPANION COURSE AT FIRMSCONSULTING.COM/STRATEGYJOURNAL

THE STRATEGY JOURNAL

step q: COMPLETE THE CASE STUDIES

CASE STUDY #2...

Name:	Business Case / Opportunity Lessons
Issues Studied	
	Implementation Lessons
Outcome	
	Strategy Lessons
Key Lessons	

NOTES

THE STRATEGY JOURNAL

step r: COMPLETE THE CASE STUDIES

CASE STUDY #3...

Name:	Business Case / Opportunity Lessons
Issues Studied	Implementation Lessons
Outcome	Strategy Lessons
Key Lessons	

NOTES

THE STRATEGY JOURNAL

step 5: PREPARE THE SLIDES FOR THE 2ND EXECUTIVE UPDATE

TOP 2 MESSAGES PER SECTION

BROAD FINANCIAL ANALYSES + BENCHMARKS	SPECIFIC TO PROBLEM STATEMENT FINANCIAL ANALYSES + BENCHMARKS	CASE STUDY
PROFITS	Hypothesis / Data to support hypothesis	CASE STUDY #1
OVERALL	Hypothesis / Data to support hypothesis	CASE STUDY #2
PRODUCT	Hypothesis / Data to support hypothesis	CASE STUDY #3
REGION	Hypothesis / Data to support hypothesis	
CASH ON HAND / SOLVENCY / INVESTMENTS	Hypothesis / Data to support hypothesis	
	Hypothesis / Data to support hypothesis	

RESERVE YOUR SPOT. FREE EX-MCK PARTNER EPISODES AT FIRMSCONSULTING.COM/PROMO

THE STRATEGY JOURNAL

step t: HOLD YOUR WEEKLY TEAM UPDATE

OBJECTIVE | SCHEDULE | TEMPERATURE LAST WEEK | TEMPERATURE THIS WEEK

Consultant:

Client:

Sponsor:

Champion:

Client Team Member:

ACCOMPLISHMENTS

KEY ISSUES

KEY NEXT STEPS….FROM TODAY
WHAT   WHO   WHEN

IMPLEMENTATION ISSUES

KEY NEXT STEPS….FROM PREVIOUS MEETING
WHAT   WHO   WHEN

Concern | Normal | Positive

THE STRATEGY JOURNAL

NOTES

THE 2ND CLIENT UPDATE

week 4

OF THE STUDY

THE STRATEGY JOURNAL

Date _____ / _____ / _____

Week #4

START YOUR DAY

To complete my critical path work, today people owe me…

To complete my critical path work, today I owe people…

END YOUR DAY

The potential opportunities I have identified for the benefits case are…

PRE-PRESENTING

I will ensure there are no surprises for the client, and the update meeting leads to a decision by pre-presenting the final draft update 2 slides THIS WEEK to the following clients: …

WEEK #4
Monday

WEEK 0 + 1	WEEK 2	WEEK 3	WEEK 4	WEEK 5	WEEK 6	WEEK 7	WEEK 8
	Update 1			Update 2		Update 3	Update 4
Charter ☐				Finish hypotheses testing ☐		Implement quick wins ☐	
Timelines ☐				Develop opportunities ☐		Bank benefits ☐	
Project logic ☐				Convert opportunities to benefits ☐		Finalize the size of the prize ☐	
Expectations exchange ☐				Validate the size of the prize ☐		Implementation plan ☐	
Hypotheses ☐	Financial analyses ☐			Identify quick wins ☐			
Storyboard ☐	Benchmarks ☐			Validate problems ☐			
Focus interview prep ☐	Case studies ☐			Options to address problems ☐			
	Range of the size of the prize ☐						
Knowledge capture planning ☐	Start testing hypotheses ☐						

THE STRATEGY JOURNAL

Week #4

NOTES

WEEK #4
Monday

THE STRATEGY JOURNAL

Date _____ / _____ / _____   **Week #4**

START YOUR DAY

To complete my critical path work, today people owe me…

To complete my critical path work, today I owe people…

END YOUR DAY

The potential opportunities I have identified for the benefits case are…

DELIGHTING MY CLIENT

I realize it is not my right to serve this client and will demonstrate to the client that I understand it is a privilege to serve them today by…

WEEK #4

Tuesday

WEEK 0 + 1	WEEK 2	WEEK 3	WEEK 4	WEEK 5	WEEK 6	WEEK 7	WEEK 8
	Update 1			Update 2		Update 3	Update 4
				Finish hypotheses testing ☐			
Charter ☐				Develop opportunities ☐		Implement quick wins ☐	
Timelines ☐				Convert opportunities to benefits ☐		Bank benefits ☐	
Project logic ☐				Validate the size of the prize ☐		Finalize the size of the prize ☐	
Expectations exchange ☐				Identify quick wins ☐		Implementation plan ☐	
Hypotheses ☐	Financial analyses		☐	Validate problems ☐			
Storyboard ☐	Benchmarks		☐	Options to address problems ☐			
Focus interview prep ☐	Case studies		☐				
	Range of the size of the prize		☐				
Knowledge capture planning ☐	Start testing hypotheses		☐				

THE STRATEGY JOURNAL

Week #4

NOTES

> **WEEK #4**
> *Tuesday*

THE STRATEGY JOURNAL

Date _____ / _____ / _____   **Week #4**

START YOUR DAY

| To complete my critical path work, today people owe me... | To complete my critical path work, today I owe people... |

END YOUR DAY

The potential opportunities I have identified for the benefits case are...

DELIGHTING MY CLIENT

I realize it is not my right to serve this client and will demonstrate to the client that I understand it is a privilege to serve them today by...

WEEK #4
Wednesday

WEEK 0 + 1	WEEK 2	WEEK 3	WEEK 4	WEEK 5	WEEK 6	WEEK 7	WEEK 8
	Update 1			Update 2		Update 3	Update 4
Charter ☐				Finish hypotheses testing ☐		Implement quick wins ☐	
Timelines ☐				Develop opportunities ☐		Bank benefits ☐	
Project logic ☐				Convert opportunities to benefits ☐		Finalize the size of the prize ☐	
Expectations exchange ☐				Validate the size of the prize ☐		Implementation plan ☐	
Hypotheses ☐	Financial analyses ☐			Identify quick wins ☐			
Storyboard ☐	Benchmarks ☐			Validate problems ☐			
Focus interview prep ☐	Case studies ☐			Options to address problems ☐			
	Range of the size of the prize ☐						
Knowledge capture planning ☐	Start testing hypotheses ☐						

THE STRATEGY JOURNAL

Week #4

NOTES

WEEK #4
Wednesday

THE STRATEGY JOURNAL

Date ____ / ____ / _____

Week #4

START YOUR DAY

To complete my critical path work, today people owe me...

To complete my critical path work, today I owe people...

END YOUR DAY

The potential opportunities I have identified for the benefits case are...

DELIGHTING MY CLIENT

I realize it is not my right to serve this client and will demonstrate to the client that I understand it is a privilege to serve them today by...

WEEK #4
Thursday

WEEK 0 + 1	WEEK 2	WEEK 3	WEEK 4	WEEK 5	WEEK 6	WEEK 7	WEEK 8
	Update 1			Update 2		Update 3	Update 4
Charter ☐				Finish hypotheses testing ☐		Implement quick wins ☐	
Timelines ☐				Develop opportunities ☐		Bank benefits ☐	
Project logic ☐				Convert opportunities to benefits ☐		Finalize the size of the prize ☐	
Expectations exchange ☐				Validate the size of the prize ☐		Implementation plan ☐	
Hypotheses ☐	Financial analyses ☐			Identify quick wins ☐			
Storyboard ☐	Benchmarks ☐			Validate problems ☐			
Focus interview prep ☐	Case studies ☐			Options to address problems ☐			
	Range of the size of the prize ☐						
Knowledge capture planning ☐	Start testing hypotheses ☐						

Week #4

NOTES

WEEK #4
Thursday

THE STRATEGY JOURNAL

Date ____ / ____ / _____   **Week #4**

START YOUR DAY

| To complete my critical path work, today people owe me... | To complete my critical path work, today I owe people... |

END YOUR DAY

The potential opportunities I have identified for the benefits case are...

FINAL UPDATES FOR 2ND CLIENT UPDATE

I have allocated enough time to update, check, and recheck the presentation for the 2nd client update and am confident it will be a success because...

WEEK #4
Friday

WEEK 0 + 1	WEEK 2	WEEK 3	WEEK 4	WEEK 5	WEEK 6	WEEK 7	WEEK 8
	Update 1			Update 2		Update 3	Update 4
Charter				Finish hypotheses testing		Implement quick wins	
Timelines				Develop opportunities		Bank benefits	
Project logic				Convert opportunities to benefits		Finalize the size of the prize	
Expectations exchange				Validate the size of the prize		Implementation plan	
Hypotheses	Financial analyses			Identify quick wins			
Storyboard	Benchmarks			Validate problems			
Focus interview prep	Case studies			Options to address problems			
	Range of the size of the prize						
Knowledge capture planning	Start testing hypotheses						

THE STRATEGY JOURNAL

Week #4

NOTES

WEEK #4

Friday

THE STRATEGY JOURNAL

step u: ACT ON THE NEXT STEPS FROM THE 2ND EXECUTIVE UPDATE

SECTIONS IN THE UPDATE

WHERE WE ARE
Show 4 slides
1. Slide: Problem statement + tree.
2. Slide: Timeline.
3. Slide: Charter.
4. Slide: 3 most important messages you will deliver today.

REVIEW WHAT WE FOUND IN FOCUS INTERVIEWS
Show 2 slides
1. Most important finding #1.
2. Most important finding #2.

FINANCIAL ANALYSES
Show 4-6 slides
1. What are the problem areas you will investigate further?
2. Tell a story.

BENCHMARKS
Show 2-3 slides
1. What is the estimated range of benefits if the client was more in line with peers?
2. What will need to be tested further?

CASE STUDIES
1. 1 slide per case study.
2. What is the most important reason the initiatives profiled failed/succeed?

ASK THE CLIENT TO AGREE TO A DECISION
Show 1 slide
1. Now that we know x and y are not causing the problem to as large a degree, do we agree to focus on z?

WHAT YOU WILL SEE NEXT
1. Calculated validated benefits range.
2. Quick wins list.
3. Options to fix the problem.

KEY NEXT STEPS…. FROM 2ND CLIENT UPDATE MEETING

WHAT	WHO	WHEN

THE STRATEGY JOURNAL

step v: VALIDATE YOUR PRELIMINARY STORYBOARD

| I HAVE IDENTIFIED THE CORRECT PROBLEM AND ROOT CAUSE ISSUES IN MY PRELIMINARY STORY BOARD AS… | THE FOCUS INTERVIEW DATA CORROBORATING THESE ISSUES WITH RANKING AND QOUTES ARE… | THE FINANCIAL ANALYSIS, BENCHMARKING, AND CASE STUDY DATA CORROBORATING THESE ISSUES ARE… |

| I HAVE IDENTIFIED THE FOLLOWING NEW PROBLEMS THAT THE CLIENT SHOULD FIX… | THESE PROBLEMS ARE FINANCIALLY IMPORTANT TO THE CLIENT BECAUSE… | WITH THE OPTIONS OF CHANGING THE SCOPE OF MY CURRENT WORK OR TREATING THESE NEW PROBLEMS AS A POTENTIAL NEW STUDY, I HAVE CHOSEN TO… |

THE STRATEGY JOURNAL

step w: HOLD YOUR WEEKLY TEAM UPDATE

OBJECTIVE   SCHEDULE   TEMPERATURE LAST WEEK   TEMPERATURE THIS WEEK

Consultant:

Client:

Sponsor:

Champion:

Client Team Member:

ACCOMPLISHMENTS

KEY ISSUES

KEY NEXT STEPS….FROM TODAY
WHAT   WHO   WHEN

IMPLEMENTATION ISSUES

KEY NEXT STEPS….FROM PREVIOUS MEETING
WHAT   WHO   WHEN

Concern   Normal   Positive

FINISH TESTING
HYPOTHESES
AND GENERATE
OPPORTUNITY
CHARTS

week 5

OF THE STUDY

THE STRATEGY JOURNAL

Date _____ / _____ / _____

Week #5

START YOUR DAY

To complete my critical path work, today people owe me...

To complete my critical path work, today I owe people...

END YOUR DAY

The potential opportunities I have identified for the benefits case are...

DELIGHTING MY CLIENT

I realize it is not my right to serve this client and will demonstrate to the client that I understand it is a privilege to serve them today by...

WEEK #5

Monday

WEEK 0 - 1	WEEK 2	WEEK 3	WEEK 4	WEEK 5	WEEK 6	WEEK 7	WEEK 8
	Update 1			Update 2		Update 3	Update 4
Charter ☐				Finish hypotheses testing ☐			
Timelines ☐				Develop opportunities ☐		Implement quick wins ☐	
Project logic ☐				Convert opportunities to benefits ☐		Bank benefits ☐	
Expectations exchange ☐				Validate the size of the prize ☐		Finalize the size of the prize ☐	
Hypotheses ☐	Financial analyses ☐			Identify quick wins ☐		Implementation plan ☐	
Storyboard ☐	Benchmarks ☐			Validate problems ☐			
Focus interview prep ☐	Case studies ☐			Options to address problems ☐			
Knowledge capture planning ☐	Range of the size of the prize ☐						
	Start testing hypotheses ☐						

RESERVE YOUR SPOT. FREE EX-MCK PARTNER EPISODES AT FIRMSCONSULTING.COM/PROMO

THE STRATEGY JOURNAL

Week #5

NOTES

WEEK #5
Monday

THE STRATEGY JOURNAL

Date _____ / _____ / _____   **Week #5**

START YOUR DAY

To complete my critical path work, today people owe me…

To complete my critical path work, today I owe people…

END YOUR DAY

The potential opportunities I have identified for the benefits case are…

DELIGHTING MY CLIENT

I realize it is not my right to serve this client and will demonstrate to the client that I understand it is a privilege to serve them today by…

WEEK #5

Tuesday

WEEK 0 + 1	WEEK 2	WEEK 3	WEEK 4	WEEK 5	WEEK 6	WEEK 7	WEEK 8
	Update 1			Update 2		Update 3	Update 4
Charter				Finish hypotheses testing			
Timelines				Develop opportunities		Implement quick wins	
Project logic				Convert opportunities to benefits		Bank benefits	
Expectations exchange				Validate the size of the prize		Finalize the size of the prize	
				Identify quick wins		Implementation plan	
Hypotheses	Financial analyses			Validate problems			
Storyboard	Benchmarks			Options to address problems			
Focus interview prep	Case studies						
	Range of the size of the prize						
Knowledge capture planning	Start testing hypotheses						

138   RESERVE YOUR SPOT. FREE EX-MCK PARTNER EPISODES AT FIRMSCONSULTING.COM/PROMO

THE STRATEGY JOURNAL

Week #5

NOTES

WEEK #5

Tuesday

THE STRATEGY JOURNAL

Date ____ / ____ / _____

Week #5

START YOUR DAY

To complete my critical path work, today people owe me…

To complete my critical path work, today I owe people…

END YOUR DAY

The potential opportunities I have identified for the benefits case are…

DELIGHTING MY CLIENT

I realize it is not my right to serve this client and will demonstrate to the client that I understand it is a privilege to serve them today by…

WEEK #5

Wednesday

WEEK 0 + 1	WEEK 2	WEEK 3	WEEK 4	WEEK 5	WEEK 6	WEEK 7	WEEK 8
	Update 1			Update 2		Update 3	Update 4
Charter ☐				Finish hypotheses testing ☐			
Timelines ☐				Develop opportunities ☐		Implement quick wins ☐	
Project logic ☐				Convert opportunities to benefits ☐		Bank benefits ☐	
Expectations exchange ☐				Validate the size of the prize ☐		Finalize the size of the prize ☐	
				Identify quick wins ☐		Implementation plan ☐	
Hypotheses ☐	Financial analyses ☐			Validate problems ☐			
Storyboard ☐	Benchmarks ☐			Options to address problems ☐			
Focus interview prep ☐	Case studies ☐						
	Range of the size of the prize ☐						
Knowledge capture planning ☐	Start testing hypotheses ☐						

THE STRATEGY JOURNAL

Week #5

NOTES

WEEK #5

Wednesday

THE STRATEGY JOURNAL

Date ____ / ____ / _____   **Week #5**

START YOUR DAY

To complete my critical path work, today people owe me…

To complete my critical path work, today I owe people…

END YOUR DAY

The potential opportunities I have identified for the benefits case are…

DELIGHTING MY CLIENT

I realize it is not my right to serve this client and will demonstrate to the client that I understand it is a privilege to serve them today by…

WEEK #5

Thursday

WEEK 0 + 1	WEEK 2	WEEK 3	WEEK 4	WEEK 5	WEEK 6	WEEK 7	WEEK 8
	Update 1			Update 2		Update 3	Update 4
Charter				Finish hypotheses testing			
Timelines				Develop opportunities		Implement quick wins	
Project logic				Convert opportunities to benefits		Bank benefits	
Expectations exchange				Validate the size of the prize		Finalize the size of the prize	
Hypotheses	Financial analyses			Identify quick wins		Implementation plan	
Storyboard	Benchmarks			Validate problems			
Focus interview prep	Case studies			Options to address problems			
	Range of the size of the prize						
Knowledge capture planning	Start testing hypotheses						

THE STRATEGY JOURNAL

Week #5

NOTES

WEEK #5
Thursday

THE STRATEGY JOURNAL

Date _____ / _____ / _____ **Week #5**

START YOUR DAY

To complete my critical path work, today people owe me…

To complete my critical path work, today I owe people…

END YOUR DAY

The potential opportunities I have identified for the benefits case are…

PRE-PRESENTING

I will ensure there are no surprises for the client, and the update meeting leads to a decision by pre-presenting the final draft of the 3rd update slides to the client NEXT WEEK by…

WEEK #5
Friday

WEEK 0 + 1	WEEK 2	WEEK 3	WEEK 4	WEEK 5	WEEK 6	WEEK 7	WEEK 8
	Update 1			Update 2		Update 3	Update 4
Charter ☐				Finish hypotheses testing ☐			
Timelines ☐				Develop opportunities ☐		Implement quick wins ☐	
Project logic ☐				Convert opportunities to benefits ☐		Bank benefits ☐	
Expectations exchange ☐				Validate the size of the prize ☐		Finalize the size of the prize ☐	
Hypotheses ☐	Financial analyses ☐			Identify quick wins ☐		Implementation plan ☐	
Storyboard ☐	Benchmarks ☐			Validate problems ☐			
Focus interview prep ☐	Case studies ☐			Options to address problems ☐			
	Range of the size of the prize ☐						
Knowledge capture planning ☐	Start testing hypotheses ☐						

Week #5

NOTES

WEEK #5
Friday

THE STRATEGY JOURNAL

step x: FINISH THE ANALYSES TO TEST THE HYPOTHESES AND COMPLETE THE STORYBOARD

THE STRATEGY JOURNAL

step y: DOCUMENT AND VALIDATE OPPORTUNITY #1

Opportunity:			Created by:	
What is not working/could be improved?	Describe the opportunity?		What must we change?	
How do we know it is not working?	How is the process *currently* measured?		How good/bad is it today?	
	Measure 1 /KPI	→	Quantify	
	Measure 2 /KPI	→	Quantify	
If I change x, y, and z, the opportunity can be captured by the client.				
How good could/should the process be? (Lead: How will we know we will eventually hit our target? Lag: How do we know it worked?)	How *could/should* we measure success for this opportunity?	Targets:	High Confidence →	Stretch
	Lead/Lag KPI Measure 1	→	Quantify	→
	Lead/Lag KPI Measure 2	→	Quantify	→
	Lead/Lag KPI Measure 1	→	Quantify	→

Opportunity Sheet Developed With:

Name:		Dept./Title:		Completed:	
Name:		Dept./Title:		Completed:	

Opportunity:		Created by:	

Where in the financial statements can we track the improvement from fixing this opportunity?

- Improving the KPIs can have one (or more) of seven main financial benefits:

  Tick as relevant:
  - ☐ Sell more product
  - ☐ Sell a greater proportion of high-margin products
  - ☐ Raise prices
  - ☐ Reduce a current cost
  - ☐ Avoid a future cost
  - ☐ Eliminate the need for or (growth of) some portion of an asset (eg. premises, plant and equipment, etc.)
  - ☐ Reduce / avoid capital provisions by avoiding / reducing a risk

- How big is the revenue/cost/asset/risk base that would be impacted?

- Key assumptions in the analysis/other comments (attach calculations and sources).

- If the KPIs improved by x% and y%, how much would the benefit increase

High confidence target = x	%, $	Stretch target = y	%, $

- How quickly would the benefit be realised and what would it cost

Date (month/week)										
Benefit % realised										
Investment to realise										

- What are the top 3 risks to not realizing the benefits?

Financial Logic Developed With:

Name:		Dept./Title:		Completed:	
Name:		Dept./Title:		Completed:	

THE STRATEGY JOURNAL

step z: DOCUMENT AND VALIDATE OPPORTUNITY #2

Opportunity:		Created by:	
What is not working/could be improved?	Describe the opportunity?	What must we change?	
How do we know it is not working?	How is the process *currently* measured?	How good/bad is it today?	
	Measure 1 /KPI →	Quantify	
	Measure 2 /KPI →	Quantify	
If I change x, y, and z, the opportunity can be captured by the client.			
How good could/should the process be? (Lead: How will we know we will eventually hit our target? Lag: How do we know it worked?)	How *could/should* we measure success for this opportunity?	Targets:	High Confidence → Stretch
	Lead/Lag KPI Measure 1 →	Quantify	→
	Lead/Lag KPI Measure 2 →	Quantify	→
	Lead/Lag KPI Measure 1 →	Quantify	→

Opportunity Sheet Developed With:

Name:		Dept./Title:		Completed:	
Name:		Dept./Title:		Completed:	

Opportunity:		Created by:	

Where in the financial statements can we track the improvement from fixing this opportunity?

- Improving the KPIs can have one (or more) of seven main financial benefits:

  Tick as relevant:
  - ☐ Sell more product
  - ☐ Sell a greater proportion of high-margin products
  - ☐ Raise prices
  - ☐ Reduce a current cost
  - ☐ Avoid a future cost
  - ☐ Eliminate the need for or (growth of) some portion of an asset (eg. premises, plant and equipment, etc.)
  - ☐ Reduce / avoid capital provisions by avoiding / reducing a risk

- How big is the revenue/cost/asset/risk base that would be impacted?

- Key assumptions in the analysis/other comments (attach calculations and sources).

- If the KPIs improved by x% and y%, how much would the benefit increase

High confidence target = x	%, $	Stretch target = y	%, $

- How quickly would the benefit be realised and what would it cost

Date (month/week)										
Benefit % realised										
Investment to realise										

- What are the top 3 risks to not realizing the benefits?

Financial Logic Developed With:

Name:		Dept./Title:		Completed:	
Name:		Dept./Title:		Completed:	

THE STRATEGY JOURNAL

step aa: DOCUMENT AND VALIDATE OPPORTUNITY #3

Opportunity:		Created by:	

What is not working/could be improved?	Describe the opportunity?		What must we change?	
How do we know it is not working?	How is the process *currently* measured?		How good/bad is it today?	
	Measure 1 /KPI	→	Quantify	
	Measure 2 /KPI	→	Quantify	

If I change x, y, and z, the opportunity can be captured by the client.	

How good could/should the process be? (Lead: How will we know we will eventually hit our target? Lag: How do we know it worked?)	How *could/should* we measure success for this opportunity?		Targets:	High Confidence → Stretch
	Lead/Lag KPI Measure 1	→	Quantify	→
	Lead/Lag KPI Measure 2	→	Quantify	→
	Lead/Lag KPI Measure 1	→	Quantify	→

Opportunity Sheet Developed With:

Name:		Dept./Title:		Completed:	
Name:		Dept./Title:		Completed:	

Opportunity:		Created by:	

Where in the financial statements can we track the improvement from fixing this opportunity?

- Improving the KPIs can have one (or more) of seven main financial benefits:
  Tick as relevant:
  - [ ] Sell more product
  - [ ] Sell a greater proportion of high-margin products
  - [ ] Raise prices
  - [ ] Reduce a current cost
  - [ ] Avoid a future cost
  - [ ] Eliminate the need for or (growth of) some portion of an asset (eg. premises, plant and equipment, etc.)
  - [ ] Reduce / avoid capital provisions by avoiding / reducing a risk

- How big is the revenue/cost/asset/risk base that would be impacted?
- Key assumptions in the analysis/other comments (attach calculations and sources).

- If the KPIs improved by x% and y%, how much would the benefit increase

High confidence target = x	%, $	Stretch target = y	%, $

- How quickly would the benefit be realised and what would it cost

Date (month/week)										
Benefit % realised										
Investment to realise										

- What are the top 3 risks to not realizing the benefits?

Financial Logic Developed With:

Name:		Dept./Title:		Completed:	
Name:		Dept./Title:		Completed:	

THE STRATEGY JOURNAL

step ab: DOCUMENT AND VALIDATE OPPORTUNITY #4

Opportunity:		Created by:	
What is not working/could be improved?	Describe the opportunity?	What must we change?	

How do we know it is not working?	How is the process *currently* measured?		How good/bad is it today?	
	Measure 1 /KPI	→	Quantify	
	Measure 2 /KPI	→	Quantify	

If I change x, y, and z, the opportunity can be captured by the client.	

How good could/should the process be? (Lead: How will we know we will eventually hit our target? Lag: How do we know it worked?)	How *could/should* we measure success for this opportunity?		Targets:	High Confidence	→	Stretch
	Lead/Lag KPI Measure 1	→	Quantify		→	
	Lead/Lag KPI Measure 2	→	Quantify		→	
	Lead/Lag KPI Measure 1	→	Quantify		→	

Opportunity Sheet Developed With:

Name:		Dept./Title:		Completed:	
Name:		Dept./Title:		Completed:	

Opportunity:		Created by:	

Where in the financial statements can we track the improvement from fixing this opportunity?

- Improving the KPIs can have one (or more) of seven main financial benefits:

  Tick as relevant:
  - ☐ Sell more product
  - ☐ Sell a greater proportion of high-margin products
  - ☐ Raise prices
  - ☐ Reduce a current cost
  - ☐ Avoid a future cost
  - ☐ Eliminate the need for or (growth of) some portion of an asset (eg. premises, plant and equipment, etc.)
  - ☐ Reduce / avoid capital provisions by avoiding / reducing a risk

- How big is the revenue/cost/asset/risk base that would be impacted?

- Key assumptions in the analysis/other comments (attach calculations and sources).

- If the KPIs improved by x% and y%, how much would the benefit increase

High confidence target = x	%, $	Stretch target = y	%, $

- How quickly would the benefit be realised and what would it cost

Date (month/week)												
Benefit % realised												
Investment to realise												

- What are the top 3 risks to not realizing the benefits?

Financial Logic Developed With:

Name:		Dept./Title:		Completed:	
Name:		Dept./Title:		Completed:	

THE STRATEGY JOURNAL

step ac: DOCUMENT AND VALIDATE OPPORTUNITY #5

Opportunity:			Created by:	
What is not working/could be improved?	Describe the opportunity?		What must we change?	
How do we know it is not working?	How is the process *currently* measured?		How good/bad is it today?	
	Measure 1 /KPI	→	Quantify	
	Measure 2 /KPI	→	Quantify	
If I change x, y, and z, the opportunity can be captured by the client.				
How good could/should the process be? (Lead: How will we know we will eventually hit our target? Lag: How do we know it worked?)	How *could/should* we measure success for this opportunity?		Targets:	High Confidence → Stretch
	Lead/Lag KPI Measure 1	→	Quantify	→
	Lead/Lag KPI Measure 2	→	Quantify	→
	Lead/Lag KPI Measure 1	→	Quantify	→

Opportunity Sheet Developed With:

Name:		Dept./Title:		Completed:	
Name:		Dept./Title:		Completed:	

Opportunity:		Created by:	

Where in the financial statements can we track the improvement from fixing this opportunity?

- Improving the KPIs can have one (or more) of seven main financial benefits:
  Tick as relevant:
  - ☐ Sell more product
  - ☐ Sell a greater proportion of high-margin products
  - ☐ Raise prices
  - ☐ Reduce a current cost
  - ☐ Avoid a future cost
  - ☐ Eliminate the need for or (growth of) some portion of an asset (eg. premises, plant and equipment, etc.)
  - ☐ Reduce / avoid capital provisions by avoiding / reducing a risk

- How big is the revenue/cost/asset/risk base that would be impacted?

- Key assumptions in the analysis/other comments (attach calculations and sources).

- If the KPIs improved by x% and y%, how much would the benefit increase

High confidence target = x	%, $	Stretch target = y	%, $

- How quickly would the benefit be realised and what would it cost

Date (month/week)										
Benefit % realised										
Investment to realise										

- What are the top 3 risks to not realizing the benefits?

Financial Logic Developed With:

Name:		Dept./Title:		Completed:	
Name:		Dept./Title:		Completed:	

THE STRATEGY JOURNAL

step ad: DOCUMENT AND VALIDATE OPPORTUNITY #6

Opportunity:		Created by:	
What is not working/could be improved?	Describe the opportunity?	What must we change?	

How do we know it is not working?	How is the process *currently* measured?		How good/bad is it today?	
	Measure 1 /KPI	→	Quantify	
	Measure 2 /KPI	→	Quantify	

If I change x, y, and z, the opportunity can be captured by the client.	

How good could/should the process be? (Lead: How will we know we will eventually hit our target? Lag: How do we know it worked?)	How *could/should* we measure success for this opportunity?		Targets:	High Confidence	→	Stretch
	Lead/Lag KPI Measure 1	→	Quantify		→	
	Lead/Lag KPI Measure 2	→	Quantify		→	
	Lead/Lag KPI Measure 1	→	Quantify		→	

Opportunity Sheet Developed With:

Name:		Dept./Title:		Completed:	
Name:		Dept./Title:		Completed:	

Opportunity:		Created by:	

Where in the financial statements can we track the improvement from fixing this opportunity?

- Improving the KPIs can have one (or more) of seven main financial benefits:
  Tick as relevant:
  - ☐ Sell more product
  - ☐ Sell a greater proportion of high-margin products
  - ☐ Raise prices
  - ☐ Reduce a current cost
  - ☐ Avoid a future cost
  - ☐ Eliminate the need for or (growth of) some portion of an asset (eg. premises, plant and equipment, etc.)
  - ☐ Reduce / avoid capital provisions by avoiding / reducing a risk

- How big is the revenue/cost/asset/risk base that would be impacted?
- Key assumptions in the analysis/other comments (attach calculations and sources).

- If the KPIs improved by x% and y%, how much would the benefit increase

High confidence target = x	%, $	Stretch target = y	%, $

- How quickly would the benefit be realised and what would it cost

Date (month/week)										
Benefit % realised										
Investment to realise										

- What are the top 3 risks to not realizing the benefits?

Financial Logic Developed With:

Name:		Dept./Title:		Completed:	
Name:		Dept./Title:		Completed:	

THE STRATEGY JOURNAL

step ae: DOCUMENT AND VALIDATE OPPORTUNITY #7

Opportunity:			Created by:	
What is not working/could be improved?	Describe the opportunity?		What must we change?	
How do we know it is not working?	How is the process *currently* measured?		How good/bad is it today?	
	Measure 1 /KPI	→ Quantify		
	Measure 2 /KPI	→ Quantify		

If I change x, y, and z, the opportunity can be captured by the client.	

How good could/should the process be? (Lead: How will we know we will eventually hit our target? Lag: How do we know it worked?)	How *could/should* we measure success for this opportunity?		Targets:	High Confidence → Stretch
	Lead/Lag KPI Measure 1	→	Quantify	→
	Lead/Lag KPI Measure 2	→	Quantify	→
	Lead/Lag KPI Measure 1	→	Quantify	→

Opportunity Sheet Developed With:

Name:		Dept./Title:		Completed:	
Name:		Dept./Title:		Completed:	

Opportunity:			Created by:	

Where in the financial statements can we track the improvement from fixing this opportunity?

- Improving the KPIs can have one (or more) of seven main financial benefits:

  Tick as relevant:
  - ☐ Sell more product
  - ☐ Sell a greater proportion of high-margin products
  - ☐ Raise prices
  - ☐ Reduce a current cost
  - ☐ Avoid a future cost
  - ☐ Eliminate the need for or (growth of) some portion of an asset (eg. premises, plant and equipment, etc.)
  - ☐ Reduce / avoid capital provisions by avoiding / reducing a risk

- How big is the revenue/cost/asset/risk base that would be impacted?

- Key assumptions in the analysis/other comments (attach calculations and sources).

- If the KPIs improved by x% and y%, how much would the benefit increase

High confidence target = x	%, $	Stretch target = y	%, $

- How quickly would the benefit be realised and what would it cost

Date (month/week)										
Benefit % realised										
Investment to realise										

- What are the top 3 risks to not realizing the benefits?

Financial Logic Developed With:

Name:		Dept./Title:		Completed:	
Name:		Dept./Title:		Completed:	

THE STRATEGY JOURNAL

step af: DOCUMENT AND VALIDATE OPPORTUNITY #8

Opportunity:		Created by:	
What is not working/could be improved?	**Describe the opportunity?**	**What must we change?**	

How do we know it is not working?	How is the process *currently* measured?		How good/bad is it today?	
	Measure 1 /KPI	→	Quantify	
	Measure 2 /KPI	→	Quantify	

If I change x, y, and z, the opportunity can be captured by the client.	

How good could/should the process be? (Lead: How will we know we will eventually hit our target? Lag: How do we know it worked?)	How *could/should* we measure success for this opportunity?		Targets:	High Confidence	→	Stretch
	Lead/Lag KPI Measure 1	→	Quantify		→	
	Lead/Lag KPI Measure 2	→	Quantify		→	
	Lead/Lag KPI Measure 1	→	Quantify		→	

Opportunity Sheet Developed With:

Name:		Dept./Title:		Completed:	
Name:		Dept./Title:		Completed:	

Opportunity:		Created by:	

Where in the financial statements can we track the improvement from fixing this opportunity?

- Improving the KPIs can have one (or more) of seven main financial benefits:

  Tick as relevant:
  - ☐ Sell more product
  - ☐ Sell a greater proportion of high-margin products
  - ☐ Raise prices
  - ☐ Reduce a current cost
  - ☐ Avoid a future cost
  - ☐ Eliminate the need for or (growth of) some portion of an asset (eg. premises, plant and equipment, etc.)
  - ☐ Reduce / avoid capital provisions by avoiding / reducing a risk

- How big is the revenue/cost/asset/risk base that would be impacted?

- Key assumptions in the analysis/other comments (attach calculations and sources).

- If the KPIs improved by x% and y%, how much would the benefit increase

High confidence target = x	%, $	Stretch target = y	%, $

- How quickly would the benefit be realised and what would it cost

Date (month/week)										
Benefit % realised										
Investment to realise										

- What are the top 3 risks to not realizing the benefits?

Financial Logic Developed With:

Name:		Dept./Title:		Completed:	
Name:		Dept./Title:		Completed:	

THE STRATEGY JOURNAL

step ag: DOCUMENT AND VALIDATE OPPORTUNITY #9

Opportunity:		Created by:	
What is not working/could be improved?	**Describe the opportunity?**	**What must we change?**	

How do we know it is not working?	**How is the process *currently* measured?**		**How good/bad is it today?**	
	Measure 1 /KPI	→	Quantify	
	Measure 2 /KPI	→	Quantify	

If I change x, y, and z, the opportunity can be captured by the client.	

How good could/should the process be? (Lead: How will we know we will eventually hit our target? Lag: How do we know it worked?)	**How *could/should* we measure success for this opportunity?**		**Targets:**	**High Confidence**	→	**Stretch**
	Lead/Lag KPI Measure 1	→	Quantify		→	
	Lead/Lag KPI Measure 2	→	Quantify		→	
	Lead/Lag KPI Measure 1	→	Quantify		→	

Opportunity Sheet Developed With:

Name:		Dept./Title:		Completed:	
Name:		Dept./Title:		Completed:	

Opportunity:		Created by:	

Where in the financial statements can we track the improvement from fixing this opportunity?

- Improving the KPIs can have one (or more) of seven main financial benefits:
  - Tick as relevant:
    - ☐ Sell more product
    - ☐ Sell a greater proportion of high-margin products
    - ☐ Raise prices
    - ☐ Reduce a current cost
    - ☐ Avoid a future cost
    - ☐ Eliminate the need for or (growth of) some portion of an asset (eg. premises, plant and equipment, etc.)
    - ☐ Reduce / avoid capital provisions by avoiding / reducing a risk

- How big is the revenue/cost/asset/risk base that would be impacted?
- Key assumptions in the analysis/other comments (attach calculations and sources).

- If the KPIs improved by x% and y%, how much would the benefit increase

High confidence target = x	%, $	Stretch target = y	%, $

- How quickly would the benefit be realised and what would it cost

Date (month/week)										
Benefit % realised										
Investment to realise										

- What are the top 3 risks to not realizing the benefits?

Financial Logic Developed With:

Name:		Dept./Title:		Completed:	
Name:		Dept./Title:		Completed:	

THE STRATEGY JOURNAL

step ah: DOCUMENT AND VALIDATE OPPORTUNITY #10

Opportunity:		Created by:	
What is not working/could be improved?	Describe the opportunity?	What must we change?	
How do we know it is not working?	How is the process *currently* measured?	How good/bad is it today?	
	Measure 1 /KPI →	Quantify	
	Measure 2 /KPI →	Quantify	
If I change x, y, and z, the opportunity can be captured by the client.			
How good could/should the process be? (Lead: How will we know we will eventually hit our target? Lag: How do we know it worked?)	How could/should we measure success for this opportunity?	Targets:	High Confidence → Stretch
	Lead/Lag KPI Measure 1 →	Quantify	→
	Lead/Lag KPI Measure 2 →	Quantify	→
	Lead/Lag KPI Measure 1 →	Quantify	→

Opportunity Sheet Developed With:

Name:		Dept./Title:		Completed:	
Name:		Dept./Title:		Completed:	

Opportunity:		Created by:	

Where in the financial statements can we track the improvement from fixing this opportunity?

- Improving the KPIs can have one (or more) of seven main financial benefits:
  Tick as relevant:
  - ☐ Sell more product
  - ☐ Sell a greater proportion of high-margin products
  - ☐ Raise prices
  - ☐ Reduce a current cost
  - ☐ Avoid a future cost
  - ☐ Eliminate the need for or (growth of) some portion of an asset (eg. premises, plant and equipment, etc.)
  - ☐ Reduce / avoid capital provisions by avoiding / reducing a risk

- How big is the revenue/cost/asset/risk base that would be impacted?
- Key assumptions in the analysis/other comments (attach calculations and sources).

- If the KPIs improved by x% and y%, how much would the benefit increase

High confidence target = x	%, $	Stretch target = y	%, $

- How quickly would the benefit be realised and what would it cost

Date (month/week)										
Benefit % realised										
Investment to realise										

- What are the top 3 risks to not realizing the benefits?

Financial Logic Developed With:

Name:		Dept./Title:		Completed:	
Name:		Dept./Title:		Completed:	

THE STRATEGY JOURNAL

step ai: HOLD YOUR WEEKLY TEAM UPDATE

OBJECTIVE   SCHEDULE   TEMPERATURE LAST WEEK   TEMPERATURE THIS WEEK

Consultant:

Client:

Sponsor:

Champion:

Client Team Member:

ACCOMPLISHMENTS

KEY ISSUES

KEY NEXT STEPS….FROM TODAY
WHAT   WHO   WHEN

IMPLEMENTATION ISSUES

KEY NEXT STEPS….FROM PREVIOUS MEETING
WHAT   WHO   WHEN

Concern   Normal   Positive

NOTES

THE 3ʳᵈ CLIENT UPDATE

week 6

OF THE STUDY

THE STRATEGY JOURNAL

Date _____ / _____ / _____

Week #6

START YOUR DAY

To complete my critical path work, today people owe me...

To complete my critical path work, today I owe people...

END YOUR DAY

The potential opportunities I have identified for the benefits case are...

DELIGHTING MY CLIENT

I will ensure there are no surprises for the client, and the update meeting leads to a decision by pre-presenting the final draft update 3 slides to the client THIS WEEK by ...

WEEK #6

Monday

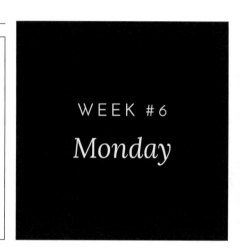

WEEK 0 + 1	WEEK 2	WEEK 3	WEEK 4	WEEK 5	WEEK 6	WEEK 7	WEEK 8
	Update 1			Update 2		Update 3	Update 4
Charter ☐				Finish hypotheses testing ☐		Implement quick wins ☐	
Timelines ☐				Develop opportunities ☐		Bank benefits ☐	
Project logic ☐				Convert opportunities to benefits ☐		Finalize the size of the prize ☐	
Expectations exchange ☐				Validate the size of the prize ☐		Implementation plan ☐	
Hypotheses ☐	Financial analyses ☐			Identify quick wins ☐			
Storyboard ☐	Benchmarks ☐			Validate problems ☐			
Focus interview prep ☐	Case studies ☐			Options to address problems ☐			
	Range of the size of the prize ☐						
Knowledge capture planning ☐	Start testing hypotheses ☐						

– THE STRATEGY JOURNAL

Week #6

NOTES

WEEK #6
Monday

THE STRATEGY JOURNAL

step aj: PREPARE THE SLIDES FOR THE 3ᴿᴰ EXECUTIVE UPDATE

SECTIONS IN THE UPDATE

WHERE WE ARE

Show 4 slides
1. Slide: Problem statement + tree.
2. Slide: Timeline.
3. Slide: Charter.
4. Slide: 3 most important messages you will deliver today. This is the executive summary.

REVIEW WHAT WE FOUND IN OUR ANALYSES

Show the main storyboard: 5 – 10 slides
1. Tight and focused story.

VALIDATING THE BENEFITS CASE

Show 4-6 slides
1. Slide: All benefits on matrix: size vs. ease of implementation.
2. Slide: Net benefit of all benefits minus investment costs.
3. Slides on 3 top benefits.
4. List of quick wins + net benefits.

OPTIONS FOR CLIENT

Show 4 slides
1. Slide: All options.
2. Slide: Trade-offs option 1.
3. Slide: Trade-offs option 2.
4. Slide: Trade-offs option 3.
5. Showing each option on a separate slide is optional.

ASK THE CLIENT TO AGREE TO A DECISION

Show 1 slide
1. Do we agree that Option 3 is the option we will analyze going forward?

INITIAL IMPLEMENTATION PLAN

1. Slide: Quick wins timeline.
2. Slide: Planning implementation.

WHAT YOU WILL SEE NEXT

1. Updated benefits case with selected option.
2. Revised implementation plan.
3. Revised quick wins and initial results.

WHAT HAPPENS NEXT

The 3ʳᵈ update is your final update. Not much will change after this update. So what is the purpose of the 4ᵗʰ update?

The 10 working days before the 4ᵗʰ update is a time to meet as many key executives as possible to ensure they understand the benefits case for implementing the recommendations. Therefore, the 4ᵗʰ update is one where the client is effectively agreeing to the smaller first implementation phase.

Implementation should begin for the quick wins **before** the 4ᵗʰ update. In the next 10 days you want at least 1 but preferably 2 quick wins **implemented** so that you can present them in the 4ᵗʰ update. At least a few quick wins can be easily implemented without requiring senior approval, so this will be possible.

Presenting a quick win that has been implemented by employees with a verified benefits creates momentum by moving the study from planning to reality. Most consultants struggle with this transition and wait for the implementation phase to be approved. This delays the process and often offers rival consulting firms an opportunity to bid for implementation phase. By generating results from the quick wins, and banking some benefits, the client is more likely to start the implementation phase immediately to avoid losing this momentum.

NOTES

THE STRATEGY JOURNAL

Date _____ / _____ / _____   **Week #6**

START YOUR DAY

To complete my critical path work, today people owe me...

To complete my critical path work, today I owe people...

END YOUR DAY

The potential opportunities I have identified for the benefits case are...

DELIGHTING MY CLIENT

I realize it is not my right to serve this client and will demonstrate to the client that I understand it is a privilege to serve them today by...

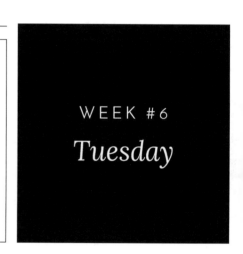

WEEK #6

Tuesday

WEEK 0 + 1	WEEK 2	WEEK 3	WEEK 4	WEEK 5	WEEK 6	WEEK 7	WEEK 8
	Update 1			Update 2		Update 3	Update 4
Charter				Finish hypotheses testing			
Timelines				Develop opportunities		Implement quick wins	
Project logic				Convert opportunities to benefits		Bank benefits	
Expectations exchange				Validate the size of the prize		Finalize the size of the prize	
Hypotheses	Financial analyses			Identify quick wins		Implementation plan	
Storyboard	Benchmarks			Validate problems			
Focus interview prep	Case studies			Options to address problems			
	Range of the size of the prize						
Knowledge capture planning	Start testing hypotheses						

164   RESERVE YOUR SPOT. FREE EX-MCK PARTNER EPISODES AT FIRMSCONSULTING.COM/PROMO

THE STRATEGY JOURNAL

Week #6

NOTES

WEEK #6
Tuesday

THE STRATEGY JOURNAL

Date _____ / _____ / _____

Week #6

START YOUR DAY

To complete my critical path work, today people owe me...

To complete my critical path work, today I owe people...

END YOUR DAY

The potential opportunities I have identified for the benefits case are...

DELIGHTING MY CLIENT

I realize it is not my right to serve this client and will demonstrate to the client that I understand it is a privilege to serve them today by...

WEEK #6

Wednesday

WEEK 0 + 1	WEEK 2	WEEK 3	WEEK 4	WEEK 5	WEEK 6	WEEK 7	WEEK 8
	Update 1			Update 2		Update 3	Update 4
Charter ☐				Finish hypotheses testing ☐		Implement quick wins ☐	
Timelines ☐				Develop opportunities ☐		Bank benefits ☐	
Project logic ☐				Convert opportunities to benefits ☐		Finalize the size of the prize ☐	
Expectations exchange ☐				Validate the size of the prize ☐		Implementation plan ☐	
Hypotheses ☐	Financial analyses ☐			Identify quick wins ☐			
Storyboard ☐	Benchmarks ☐			Validate problems ☐			
Focus interview prep ☐	Case studies ☐			Options to address problems ☐			
Knowledge capture planning ☐	Range of the size of the prize ☐						
	Start testing hypotheses ☐						

THE STRATEGY JOURNAL

Week #6

NOTES

WEEK #6
Wednesday

THE STRATEGY JOURNAL

Date _____ / _____ / _____

Week #6

START YOUR DAY

To complete my critical path work, today people owe me…

To complete my critical path work, today I owe people…

END YOUR DAY

The potential opportunities I have identified for the benefits case are…

DELIGHTING MY CLIENT

I realize it is not my right to serve this client and will demonstrate to the client that I understand it is a privilege to serve them today by…

WEEK #6

Thursday

WEEK 0 + 1	WEEK 2	WEEK 3	WEEK 4	WEEK 5	WEEK 6	WEEK 7	WEEK 8
	Update 1			Update 2		Update 3	Update 4
Charter ☐				Finish hypotheses testing ☐		Implement quick wins ☐	
Timelines ☐				Develop opportunities ☐		Bank benefits ☐	
Project logic ☐				Convert opportunities to benefits ☐		Finalize the size of the prize ☐	
Expectations exchange ☐				Validate the size of the prize ☐		Implementation plan ☐	
Hypotheses ☐	Financial analyses ☐			Identify quick wins ☐			
Storyboard ☐	Benchmarks ☐			Validate problems ☐			
Focus interview prep ☐	Case studies ☐			Options to address problems ☐			
	Range of the size of the prize ☐						
Knowledge capture planning ☐	Start testing hypotheses ☐						

RESERVE YOUR SPOT. FREE EX-MCK PARTNER EPISODES AT FIRMSCONSULTING.COM/PROMO

THE STRATEGY JOURNAL

Week #6

NOTES

WEEK #6
Thursday

THE STRATEGY JOURNAL

Date _____ / _____ / _____

Week #6

START YOUR DAY

To complete my critical path work, today people owe me…

To complete my critical path work, today I owe people…

END YOUR DAY

The potential opportunities I have identified for the benefits case are…

3ʳᴅ CLIENT UPDATE

I have allocated enough time to update, check, and recheck the 3rd client update presentation by…

WEEK #6

Friday

WEEK 0 + 1	WEEK 2	WEEK 3	WEEK 4	WEEK 5	WEEK 6	WEEK 7	WEEK 8
	Update 1			Update 2		Update 3	Update 4
Charter ☐				Finish hypotheses testing ☐		Implement quick wins ☐	
Timelines ☐				Develop opportunities ☐		Bank benefits ☐	
Project logic ☐				Convert opportunities to benefits ☐		Finalize the size of the prize ☐	
Expectations exchange ☐				Validate the size of the prize ☐		Implementation plan ☐	
Hypotheses ☐	Financial analyses ☐			Identify quick wins ☐			
Storyboard ☐	Benchmarks ☐			Validate problems ☐			
Focus interview prep ☐	Case studies ☐			Options to address problems ☐			
	Range of the size of the prize ☐						
Knowledge capture planning ☐	Start testing hypotheses ☐						

THE STRATEGY JOURNAL

Week #6

NOTES

WEEK #6
Friday

step ak: ACT ON THE NEXT STEPS FROM THE 3RD EXECUTIVE UPDATE

SECTIONS IN THE UPDATE

WHERE WE ARE

Show 4 slides
1. Slide: Problem statement + tree.
2. Slide: Timeline.
3. Slide: Charter.
4. Slide: 3 most important messages you will deliver today. This is the executive summary.

REVIEW WHAT WE FOUND IN OUR ANALYSES

Show the main storyboard: 5 – 10 slides
1. Tight and focused story.

VALIDATING THE BENEFITS CASE

Show 4-6 slides
1. Slide: All benefits on matrix: size vs. ease of implementation.
2. Slide: Net benefit of all benefits minus investment costs.
3. Slides on 3 top benefits.
4. List of quick wins + net benefits.

OPTIONS FOR CLIENT

Show 4 slides
1. Slide: All options.
2. Slide: Trade-offs option 1.
3. Slide: Trade-offs option 2.
4. Slide: Trade-offs option 3.
5. Showing each option on a separate slide is optional.

ASK THE CLIENT TO AGREE TO A DECISION

Show 1 slide
1. Do we agree that Option 3 is the option we will analyze going forward?

INITIAL IMPLEMENTATION PLAN

1. Slide: Quick wins timeline.
2. Slide: Planning implementation.

WHAT YOU WILL SEE NEXT

1. Updated benefits case with selected option.
2. Revised implementation plan.
3. Revised quick wins and initial results.

KEY NEXT STEPS…. FROM 3RD CLIENT UPDATE MEETING

WHAT	WHO	WHEN

THE STRATEGY JOURNAL

step a1: HOLD YOUR WEEKLY TEAM UPDATE

OBJECTIVE	SCHEDULE	TEMPERATURE LAST WEEK	TEMPERATURE THIS WEEK

Consultant:

Client:

Sponsor:

Champion:

Client Team Member:

ACCOMPLISHMENTS

KEY ISSUES

KEY NEXT STEPS….FROM TODAY
WHAT   WHO   WHEN

IMPLEMENTATION ISSUES

KEY NEXT STEPS….FROM PREVIOUS MEETING
WHAT   WHO   WHEN

| Concern | Normal | Positive |

FREE EPISODE FROM BOOK'S COMPANION COURSE AT FIRMSCONSULTING.COM/STRATEGYJOURNAL

THE STRATEGY JOURNAL

NOTES

START THE
QUICK WINS
IMPLEMENTATION

week 7

OF THE STUDY

THE STRATEGY JOURNAL

Date _____ / _____ / _____   **Week #7**

START YOUR DAY

| To complete my critical path work, today people owe me… | To complete my critical path work, today I owe people… |

END YOUR DAY

I will remove the roadblocks to implementing the quick wins by…

IMPLEMENTATION

I am transitioning from analysis to implementation by…

QUICK WINS

The 2-3 quick wins I will implement, validate, and pre-present before the final client update are…

I am confident they can be done in the next 10 days because…

WEEK #7
Monday

WEEK 0 + 1	WEEK 2	WEEK 3	WEEK 4	WEEK 5	WEEK 6	WEEK 7	WEEK 8
	Update 1			Update 2		**Update 3**	**Update 4**
Charter				Finish hypotheses testing		Implement quick wins	
Timelines				Develop opportunities		Bank benefits	
Project logic				Convert opportunities to benefits		Finalize the size of the prize	
Expectations exchange				Validate the size of the prize		Implementation plan	
Hypotheses	Financial analyses			Identify quick wins			
Storyboard	Benchmarks			Validate problems			
Focus interview prep	Case studies			Options to address problems			
	Range of the size of the prize						
Knowledge capture planning	Start testing hypotheses						

THE STRATEGY JOURNAL

Week #7

NOTES

WEEK #7

Monday

THE STRATEGY JOURNAL

step am: QUICK WIN #1 TO IMPLEMENT IN THE NEXT 2 WEEKS

Opportunity:			Created by:	
What is not working/could be improved?	Describe the opportunity?		What must we change?	
How do we know it is not working?	How is the process *currently* measured?		How good/bad is it today?	
	Measure 1 /KPI	→	Quantify	
	Measure 2 /KPI	→	Quantify	
If I change x, y, and z, the opportunity can be captured by the client.				
How good could/should the process be? (Lead: How will we know we will eventually hit our target? Lag: How do we know it worked?)	How *could/should* we measure success for this opportunity?		Targets:	High Confidence → Stretch
	Lead/Lag KPI Measure 1	→	Quantify	→
	Lead/Lag KPI Measure 2	→	Quantify	→
	Lead/Lag KPI Measure 1	→	Quantify	→

Opportunity Sheet Developed With:

Name:		Dept./Title:		Completed:	
Name:		Dept./Title:		Completed:	

Opportunity:			Created by:	

Where in the financial statements can we track the improvement from fixing this opportunity?

- Improving the KPIs can have one (or more) of seven main financial benefits:
  Tick as relevant:
  - ☐ Sell more product
  - ☐ Sell a greater proportion of high-margin products
  - ☐ Raise prices
  - ☐ Reduce a current cost
  - ☐ Avoid a future cost
  - ☐ Eliminate the need for or (growth of) some portion of an asset (eg. premises, plant and equipment, etc.)
  - ☐ Reduce / avoid capital provisions by avoiding / reducing a risk

- How big is the revenue/cost/asset/risk base that would be impacted?

- Key assumptions in the analysis/other comments (attach calculations and sources).

- If the KPIs improved by x% and y%, how much would the benefit increase

High confidence target = x	%, $	Stretch target = y	%, $

- How quickly would the benefit be realised and what would it cost

Date (month/week)											
Benefit % realised											
Investment to realise											

- What are the top 3 risks to not realizing the benefits?

Financial Logic Developed With:

Name:		Dept./Title:		Completed:	
Name:		Dept./Title:		Completed:	

THE STRATEGY JOURNAL

step an: QUICK WIN #2 TO IMPLEMENT IN THE NEXT 2 WEEKS

Opportunity:		Created by:	
What is not working/could be improved?	**Describe the opportunity?**	**What must we change?**	
How do we know it is not working?	How is the process *currently* measured?	How good/bad is it today?	
	Measure 1 /KPI →	Quantify	
	Measure 2 /KPI →	Quantify	
If I change x, y, and z, the opportunity can be captured by the client.			
How good could/should the process be? (Lead: How will we know we will eventually hit our target? Lag: How do we know it worked?)	How could/should we measure success for this opportunity?	Targets:	High Confidence → Stretch
	Lead/Lag KPI Measure 1 →	Quantify	→
	Lead/Lag KPI Measure 2 →	Quantify	→
	Lead/Lag KPI Measure 1 →	Quantify	→

Opportunity Sheet Developed With:

Name:		Dept./Title:		Completed:	
Name:		Dept./Title:		Completed:	

Opportunity:		Created by:	

Where in the financial statements can we track the improvement from fixing this opportunity?

- Improving the KPIs can have one (or more) of seven main financial benefits:
  Tick as relevant:
  - ☐ Sell more product
  - ☐ Sell a greater proportion of high-margin products
  - ☐ Raise prices
  - ☐ Reduce a current cost
  - ☐ Avoid a future cost
  - ☐ Eliminate the need for or (growth of) some portion of an asset (eg. premises, plant and equipment, etc.)
  - ☐ Reduce / avoid capital provisions by avoiding / reducing a risk

- How big is the revenue/cost/asset/risk base that would be impacted?

- Key assumptions in the analysis/other comments (attach calculations and sources).

- If the KPIs improved by x% and y%, how much would the benefit increase

High confidence target = x	%, $	Stretch target = y	%, $

- How quickly would the benefit be realised and what would it cost

Date (month/week)										
Benefit % realised										
Investment to realise										

- What are the top 3 risks to not realizing the benefits?

Financial Logic Developed With:

Name:		Dept./Title:		Completed:	
Name:		Dept./Title:		Completed:	

THE STRATEGY JOURNAL

step ao: QUICK WIN #3 TO IMPLEMENT IN THE NEXT 2 WEEKS

Opportunity:			Created by:	
What is not working/could be improved?	Describe the opportunity?		What must we change?	
How do we know it is not working?	How is the process *currently* measured?		How good/bad is it today?	
	Measure 1 /KPI	→ Quantify		
	Measure 2 /KPI	→ Quantify		
If I change x, y, and z, the opportunity can be captured by the client.				
How good could/should the process be? (Lead: How will we know we will eventually hit our target? Lag: How do we know it worked?)	How *could/should* we measure success for this opportunity?	Targets:	High Confidence	→ Stretch
	Lead/Lag KPI Measure 1	→ Quantify		→
	Lead/Lag KPI Measure 2	→ Quantify		→
	Lead/Lag KPI Measure 1	→ Quantify		→

Opportunity Sheet Developed With:

Name:		Dept./Title:		Completed:	
Name:		Dept./Title:		Completed:	

Opportunity:		Created by:	

Where in the financial statements can we track the improvement from fixing this opportunity?

- Improving the KPIs can have one (or more) of seven main financial benefits:

  Tick as relevant:
  - ☐ Sell more product
  - ☐ Sell a greater proportion of high-margin products
  - ☐ Raise prices
  - ☐ Reduce a current cost
  - ☐ Avoid a future cost
  - ☐ Eliminate the need for or (growth of) some portion of an asset (eg. premises, plant and equipment, etc.)
  - ☐ Reduce / avoid capital provisions by avoiding / reducing a risk

- How big is the revenue/cost/asset/risk base that would be impacted?
- Key assumptions in the analysis/other comments (attach calculations and sources).

- If the KPIs improved by x% and y%, how much would the benefit increase

High confidence target = x	%, $	Stretch target = y	%, $

- How quickly would the benefit be realised and what would it cost

Date (month/week)										
Benefit % realised										
Investment to realise										

- What are the top 3 risks to not realizing the benefits?

Financial Logic Developed With:

Name:		Dept./Title:		Completed:	
Name:		Dept./Title:		Completed:	

NOTES

THE STRATEGY JOURNAL

Date ____ / ____ / _____ **Week #7**

START YOUR DAY

To complete my critical path work, today people owe me…

To complete my critical path work, today I owe people…

END YOUR DAY

I will remove the roadblocks to implementing the quick wins by…

IMPLEMENTATION

I am transitioning from analysis to implementation by…

DELIGHTING MY CLIENT

I realize it is not my right to serve this client and will demonstrate to the client that I understand it is a privilege to serve them today by…

WEEK #7

Tuesday

WEEK 0 + 1	WEEK 2	WEEK 3	WEEK 4	WEEK 5	WEEK 6	WEEK 7	WEEK 8
	Update 1			Update 2		Update 3	Update 4
Charter ☐				Finish hypotheses testing ☐		Implement quick wins ☐	
Timelines ☐				Develop opportunities ☐		Bank benefits ☐	
Project logic ☐				Convert opportunities to benefits ☐		Finalize the size of the prize ☐	
Expectations exchange ☐				Validate the size of the prize ☐		Implementation plan ☐	
Hypotheses ☐	Financial analyses ☐			Identify quick wins ☐			
Storyboard ☐	Benchmarks ☐			Validate problems ☐			
Focus interview prep ☐	Case studies ☐			Options to address problems ☐			
	Range of the size of the prize ☐						
Knowledge capture planning ☐	Start testing hypotheses ☐						

RESERVE YOUR SPOT. FREE EX-MCK PARTNER EPISODES AT FIRMSCONSULTING.COM/PROMO

THE STRATEGY JOURNAL

Week #7

NOTES

WEEK #7
Tuesday

THE STRATEGY JOURNAL

Date _____ / _____ / _____ **Week #7**

START YOUR DAY

To complete my critical path work, today people owe me…

To complete my critical path work, today I owe people…

END YOUR DAY

I will remove the roadblocks to implementing the quick wins by…

IMPLEMENTATION

I am transitioning from analysis to implementation by…

DELIGHTING MY CLIENT

I realize it is not my right to serve this client and will demonstrate to the client that I understand it is a privilege to serve them today by…

WEEK #7

Wednesday

WEEK 0 + 1	WEEK 2	WEEK 3	WEEK 4	WEEK 5	WEEK 6	WEEK 7	WEEK 8
	Update 1			Update 2		Update 3	Update 4
Charter ☐				Finish hypotheses testing ☐		Implement quick wins ☐	
Timelines ☐				Develop opportunities ☐		Bank benefits ☐	
Project logic ☐				Convert opportunities to benefits ☐		Finalize the size of the prize ☐	
Expectations exchange ☐				Validate the size of the prize ☐		Implementation plan ☐	
Hypotheses ☐	Financial analyses ☐			Identify quick wins ☐			
Storyboard ☐	Benchmarks ☐			Validate problems ☐			
Focus interview prep ☐	Case studies ☐			Options to address problems ☐			
	Range of the size of the prize ☐						
Knowledge capture planning ☐	Start testing hypotheses ☐						

THE STRATEGY JOURNAL

Week #7

NOTES

WEEK #7
Wednesday

THE STRATEGY JOURNAL

Date ____ / ____ / _____

Week #7

START YOUR DAY

To complete my critical path work, today people owe me…

To complete my critical path work, today I owe people…

END YOUR DAY

I will remove the roadblocks to implementing the quick wins by…

IMPLEMENTATION

I am transitioning from analysis to implementation by…

DELIGHTING MY CLIENT

I realize it is not my right to serve this client and will demonstrate to the client that I understand it is a privilege to serve them today by…

WEEK #7

Thursday

WEEK 0 + 1	WEEK 2	WEEK 3	WEEK 4	WEEK 5	WEEK 6	WEEK 7	WEEK 8
	Update 1			Update 2		Update 3	Update 4
Charter ☐				Finish hypotheses testing ☐			
Timelines ☐				Develop opportunities ☐		Implement quick wins ☐	
Project logic ☐				Convert opportunities to benefits ☐		Bank benefits ☐	
Expectations exchange ☐				Validate the size of the prize ☐		Finalize the size of the prize ☐	
Hypotheses ☐	Financial analyses ☐			Identify quick wins ☐		Implementation plan ☐	
Storyboard ☐	Benchmarks ☐			Validate problems ☐			
Focus interview prep ☐	Case studies ☐			Options to address problems ☐			
	Range of the size of the prize ☐						
Knowledge capture planning ☐	Start testing hypotheses ☐						

RESERVE YOUR SPOT. FREE EX-MCK PARTNER EPISODES AT FIRMSCONSULTING.COM/PROMO

THE STRATEGY JOURNAL

Week #7

NOTES

WEEK #7

Thursday

THE STRATEGY JOURNAL

Date _____ / _____ / _____   **Week #7**

START YOUR DAY

To complete my critical path work, today people owe me...

To complete my critical path work, today I owe people...

END YOUR DAY

I will remove the roadblocks to implementing the quick wins by...

IMPLEMENTATION

I am transitioning from analysis to implementation by...

DELIGHTING MY CLIENT

I realize it is not my right to serve this client and will demonstrate to the client that I understand it is a privilege to serve them today by...

WEEK #7
Friday

WEEK 0 – 1	WEEK 2	WEEK 3	WEEK 4	WEEK 5	WEEK 6	WEEK 7	WEEK 8
	Update 1			Update 2		Update 3	Update 4
Charter ☐				Finish hypotheses testing ☐		Implement quick wins ☐	
Timelines ☐				Develop opportunities ☐		Bank benefits ☐	
Project logic ☐				Convert opportunities to benefits ☐		Finalize the size of the prize ☐	
Expectations exchange ☐				Validate the size of the prize ☐		Implementation plan ☐	
Hypotheses ☐	Financial analyses ☐			Identify quick wins ☐			
Storyboard ☐	Benchmarks ☐			Validate problems ☐			
Focus interview prep ☐	Case studies ☐			Options to address problems ☐			
	Range of the size of the prize ☐						
Knowledge capture planning ☐	Start testing hypotheses ☐						

THE STRATEGY JOURNAL

Week #7

NOTES

WEEK #7

Friday

THE STRATEGY JOURNAL

step ap: HOLD YOUR WEEKLY TEAM UPDATE

OBJECTIVE	SCHEDULE	TEMPERATURE LAST WEEK	TEMPERATURE THIS WEEK

Consultant:

Client:

Sponsor:

Champion:

Client Team Member:

ACCOMPLISHMENTS

KEY ISSUES

KEY NEXT STEPS….FROM TODAY
WHAT   WHO   WHEN

IMPLEMENTATION ISSUES

KEY NEXT STEPS….FROM PREVIOUS MEETING
WHAT   WHO   WHEN

| Concern | Normal | Positive |

PREPARING FOR THE
4TH CLIENT UPDATE
AND IMPLEMENTATION

week 8

OF THE STUDY

THE STRATEGY JOURNAL

Date _____ / _____ / _____

Week #8

START YOUR DAY | END YOUR DAY

To complete my critical path work, today people owe me…

To complete my critical path work, today I owe people…

I will remove the roadblocks to implementing the quick wins by…

IMPLEMENTATION

I know I have fully transitioned from analysis to implementation because…

PREPARING FOR THE 4ᵀᴴ AND FINAL CLIENT UPDATE

I will ensure there are no surprises for the client, and the update meeting leads to a decision by pre-presenting the final draft update 4 slides THIS WEEK to …

WEEK #8
Monday

WEEK 0 – 1	WEEK 2	WEEK 3	WEEK 4	WEEK 5	WEEK 6	WEEK 7	WEEK 8
	Update 1			Update 2		Update 3	**Update 4**
Charter				Finish hypotheses testing		Implement quick wins ☐	
Timelines				Develop opportunities		Bank benefits ☐	
Project logic				Convert opportunities to benefits		Finalize the size of the prize ☐	
Expectations exchange				Validate the size of the prize		Implementation plan ☐	
Hypotheses	Financial analyses			Identify quick wins			
Storyboard	Benchmarks			Validate problems			
Focus interview prep	Case studies			Options to address problems			
	Range of the size of the prize						
Knowledge capture planning	Start testing hypotheses						

RESERVE YOUR SPOT. FREE EX-MCK PARTNER EPISODES AT FIRMSCONSULTING.COM/PROMO

THE STRATEGY JOURNAL

Week #8

NOTES

WEEK #8

Monday

THE STRATEGY JOURNAL

step aq: PREPARING FOR THE 4TH EXECUTIVE UPDATE

SECTIONS IN THE UPDATE

WHERE WE ARE

Show 3 slides

1. Slide: Problem statement + tree.
2. Slide: Timeline.
3. Slide: 3 most important messages you will deliver today. This is the executive summary.

WHAT WE PRESENTED PREVIOUSLY

Show 5 slides

1. 3 slides on the main analysis findings.
2. Options to fix problem.
3. Net benefits of all options from the 3rd update.

REFINED BENEFITS

Show 1 slide

1. Slide showing any updates to final benefit total number.
2. There will always be some updates.

BANKED QUICK WIN BENEFITS

Show 2 slides

1. Quick wins implemented and value created for client.
2. Quick wins that can be implemented in the next month if implementation is approved.

IMPLEMENTATION PLAN

Show 1 slide

1. Implementation plan.
2. How to not lose momentum on the implementation.
3. Always show phases.

ASK THE CLIENT TO AGREE TO A DECISION

Show 1 slide

1. Do you agree to extend the engagement by 1 month to implement x benefits with verified estimates of y$?

WHAT YOU WILL SEE NEXT

Show 1 slide

1. Update on net benefit from quick wins implementation.
2. Implementation scorecard.
3. Implementation plan.

WHAT HAPPENS NEXT

The engagement blends into the implementation phase. Even when clients want a hard stop, implementation of the quick wins is usually permitted. Clients will need to, rightly, go through formal procurement processes to award a multimillion-dollar implementation phase. This will cause delays. A client is, however, usually able and willing to approve a 1-month extension to the current project, especially with a reduced team when the objectives and benefits of the 1-month extension are clear: implementing quick wins where the benefits are being validated by their own employees who are enthusiastic about the work.

By implementing some of the quick wins, client employees start to push for implementation because they see the banked benefits from the quick wins. Employees want to be a part of something that works. It helps with their performance reviews and bonuses. It helps with their promotion prospect. Therefore, employees will ask for the implementation to continue if the quick wins start generating results.

Moreover, implementation stops being '*another*' engagement the consultant is trying to sell. The implementation becomes something the company wants to do, pushed by employees. This allows the consultants to stay with the client, keep billing and work on the implementation planning.

This is different from the approach most consultants use of coming in cold and trying to create a mindset change via change management, to build momentum for implementation. This forces consultants to try to sell the idea of implementation to the employees.

This is also a different model from consultants who offer to work for free to develop the initial business case, with the goal of gaining an edge in being awarded the large and stable implementation engagement. Working for free is always a bad idea unless you have a clear strategy on how to move to billed work.

It is safer to build up a smaller implementation engagement into a larger engagement, instead of asking for the full implementation to start right at the beginning.

Like every update, asking for this extension will not be awkward because the contents have been pre-presented to all the client executives. They have had an opportunity to ask questions, understand the process, and signal their agreement. Therefore, the consultant already knows this has been approved before the update meeting.

NOTES

THE STRATEGY JOURNAL

Date _____ / _____ / _____   **Week #8**

START YOUR DAY

| To complete my critical path work, today people owe me... | To complete my critical path work, today I owe people... |

END YOUR DAY

I will remove the roadblocks to implementing the quick wins by...

IMPLEMENTATION

I know I have fully transitioned from analysis to implementation because...

DELIGHTING MY CLIENT

I realize it is not my right to serve this client and will demonstrate to the client that I understand it is a privilege to serve them today by...

WEEK #8

Tuesday

WEEK 0 + 1	WEEK 2	WEEK 3	WEEK 4	WEEK 5	WEEK 6	WEEK 7	WEEK 8
	Update 1			Update 2		Update 3	**Update 4**
Charter ☐				Finish hypotheses testing ☐		Implement quick wins ☐	
Timelines ☐				Develop opportunities ☐		Bank benefits ☐	
Project logic ☐				Convert opportunities to benefits ☐		Finalize the size of the prize ☐	
Expectations exchange ☐				Validate the size of the prize ☐		Implementation plan ☐	
Hypotheses ☐	Financial analyses ☐			Identify quick wins ☐			
Storyboard ☐	Benchmarks ☐			Validate problems ☐			
Focus interview prep ☐	Case studies ☐			Options to address problems ☐			
	Range of the size of the prize ☐						
Knowledge capture planning ☐	Start testing hypotheses ☐						

RESERVE YOUR SPOT. FREE EX-MCK PARTNER EPISODES AT FIRMSCONSULTING.COM/PROMO

THE STRATEGY JOURNAL

Week #8

NOTES

WEEK #8

Tuesday

THE STRATEGY JOURNAL

Date _____ / _____ / _____ **Week #8**

START YOUR DAY

To complete my critical path work, today people owe me...

To complete my critical path work, today I owe people...

END YOUR DAY

I will remove the roadblocks to implementing the quick wins by...

IMPLEMENTATION

I know I have fully transitioned from analysis to implementation because...

DELIGHTING MY CLIENT

I realize it is not my right to serve this client and will demonstrate to the client that I understand it is a privilege to serve them today by...

WEEK #8

Wednesday

WEEK 0 + 1	WEEK 2	WEEK 3	WEEK 4	WEEK 5	WEEK 6	WEEK 7	WEEK 8
	Update 1			Update 2		Update 3	**Update 4**
Charter ☐				Finish hypotheses testing ☐		Implement quick wins ☐	
Timelines ☐				Develop opportunities ☐		Bank benefits ☐	
Project logic ☐				Convert opportunities to benefits ☐		Finalize the size of the prize ☐	
Expectations exchange ☐				Validate the size of the prize ☐		Implementation plan ☐	
Hypotheses ☐	Financial analyses ☐			Identify quick wins ☐			
Storyboard ☐	Benchmarks ☐			Validate problems ☐			
Focus interview prep ☐	Case studies ☐			Options to address problems ☐			
	Range of the size of the prize ☐						
Knowledge capture planning ☐	Start testing hypotheses ☐						

Week #8

NOTES

WEEK #8
Wednesday

THE STRATEGY JOURNAL

Date _____ / _____ / _____   Week #8

START YOUR DAY

To complete my critical path work, today people owe me...

To complete my critical path work, today I owe people...

END YOUR DAY

I will remove the roadblocks to implementing the quick wins by...

IMPLEMENTATION

I know I have fully transitioned from analysis to implementation because...

DELIGHTING MY CLIENT

I realize it is not my right to serve this client and will demonstrate to the client that I understand it is a privilege to serve them today by...

WEEK #8
Thursday

WEEK 0+1	WEEK 2	WEEK 3	WEEK 4	WEEK 5	WEEK 6	WEEK 7	WEEK 8
	Update 1			Update 2		Update 3	Update 4
Charter ☐				Finish hypotheses testing ☐		Implement quick wins ☐	
Timelines ☐				Develop opportunities ☐		Bank benefits ☐	
Project logic ☐				Convert opportunities to benefits ☐		Finalize the size of the prize ☐	
Expectations exchange ☐				Validate the size of the prize ☐		Implementation plan ☐	
Hypotheses ☐	Financial analyses ☐			Identify quick wins ☐			
Storyboard ☐	Benchmarks ☐			Validate problems ☐			
Focus interview prep ☐	Case studies ☐			Options to address problems ☐			
	Range of the size of the prize ☐						
Knowledge capture planning ☐	Start testing hypotheses ☐						

THE STRATEGY JOURNAL

Week #8

NOTES

WEEK #8
Thursday

THE STRATEGY JOURNAL

Date _____ / _____ / _____

Week #8

START YOUR DAY

To complete my critical path work, today people owe me...

To complete my critical path work, today I owe people...

END YOUR DAY

I will remove the roadblocks to implementing the quick wins by...

IMPLEMENTATION

I know I have fully transitioned from analysis to implementation because...

DELIGHTING MY CLIENT

I realize it is not my right to serve this client and will demonstrate to the client that I understand it is a privilege to serve them today by...

WEEK #8

Friday

WEEK 0 + 1	WEEK 2	WEEK 3	WEEK 4	WEEK 5	WEEK 6	WEEK 7	WEEK 8
	Update 1			Update 2		Update 3	**Update 4**
Charter ☐				Finish hypotheses testing ☐		Implement quick wins ☐	
Timelines ☐				Develop opportunities ☐		Bank benefits ☐	
Project logic ☐				Convert opportunities to benefits ☐		Finalize the size of the prize ☐	
Expectations exchange ☐				Validate the size of the prize ☐		Implementation plan ☐	
Hypotheses ☐	Financial analyses ☐			Identify quick wins ☐			
Storyboard ☐	Benchmarks ☐			Validate problems ☐			
Focus interview prep ☐	Case studies ☐			Options to address problems ☐			
	Range of the size of the prize ☐						
Knowledge capture planning ☐	Start testing hypotheses ☐						

THE STRATEGY JOURNAL

Week #8

NOTES

WEEK #8
Friday

THE STRATEGY JOURNAL

step ar: THE 4TH EXECUTIVE UPDATE

SECTIONS IN THE UPDATE

WHERE WE ARE
Show 3 slides
1. Slide: Problem statement + tree.
2. Slide: Timeline.
3. Slide: 3 most important messages you will deliver today. This is the executive summary.

WHAT WE PRESENTED PREVIOUSLY
Show 5 slides
1. 3 slides on the main analysis findings.
2. Options to fix the problem.
3. Net benefits of all options from the 3rd update.

REFINED BENEFITS
Show 1 slide
1. Slide showing any updates to final benefit total number.
2. There will always be some updates.

BANKED QUICK WIN BENEFITS
Show 2 slides
1. Quick wins implemented and value created for client.
2. Quick wins that can be implemented in the next month if implementation is approved.

IMPLEMENTATION PLAN
Show 1 slide
1. Implementation plan.
2. How to not lose momentum on the implementation.
3. Always show phases.

ASK THE CLIENT TO AGREE TO A DECISION
Show 1 slide
1. Do you agree to extend the engagement by 1 month to implement x benefits with verified estimates of y$?

WHAT YOU WILL SEE NEXT
Show 1 slide
1. Update on net benefit from quick wins implementation.
2. Implementation scorecard.
3. Implementation plan.

KEY NEXT STEPS…. FROM 4TH CLIENT UPDATE MEETING

WHAT	WHO	WHEN

THE STRATEGY JOURNAL

step as: HOLD YOUR WEEKLY TEAM UPDATE

OBJECTIVE   SCHEDULE   TEMPERATURE LAST WEEK   TEMPERATURE THIS WEEK

Consultant:

Client:

Sponsor:

Champion:

Client Team Member:

ACCOMPLISHMENTS

KEY ISSUES

KEY NEXT STEPS….FROM TODAY
WHAT   WHO   WHEN

IMPLEMENTATION ISSUES

KEY NEXT STEPS….FROM PREVIOUS MEETING
WHAT   WHO   WHEN

Concern   Normal   Positive

END OF STUDY

THE STRATEGY JOURNAL

step at: HOW I WILL BECOME A BETTER STRATEGIST

LESSONS LEARNED

I am proud of this engagement because I added verifiable, measurable benefits to the client of...

I did a great job and will improve in the next engagement by...

I can remember several moments when I demonstrated great values and placed the needs of the client first by...

The skills that give me a competitive advantage that I need to continue developing / perfecting are...

I will improve / master these skills in the next 6 months by watching the following **StrategyTraining.com** programs...

I will know I am improving / mastering these skills by measuring...

WOULD YOU LIKE TO VIEW
EXCLUSIVE PREVIEW EPISODES
FROM THE PROGRAMS
ON THE PREVIOUS PAGE?

―――

Visit
Firmsconsulting.com/promo
to submit your email.

You will be emailed the content at no charge

―――

All content by
ex-McKinsey, BCG et al. partners.

LEARN CRITICAL THINKING

A TYPICAL MCKINSEY, BCG ET AL. ENGAGEMENT

This Journal summarizes the overall approach, slides and key steps we teach in a 270-episode video program walking through each step of a typical strategy engagement.

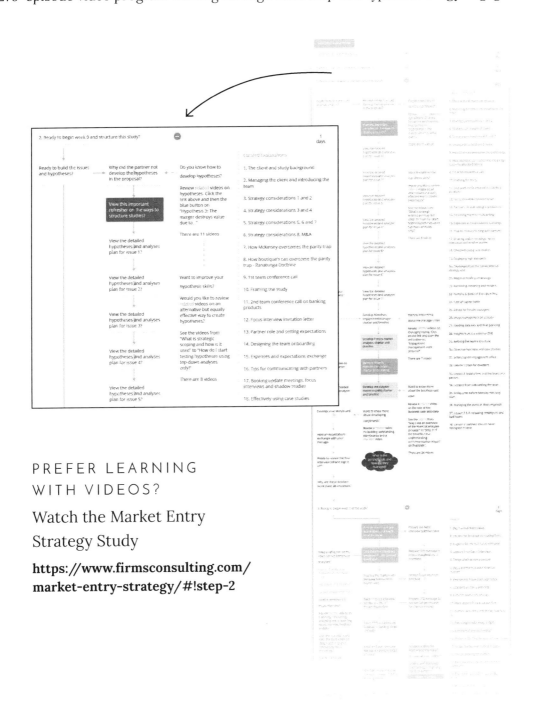

PREFER LEARNING WITH VIDEOS?

Watch the Market Entry Strategy Study

https://www.firmsconsulting.com/market-entry-strategy/#!step-2

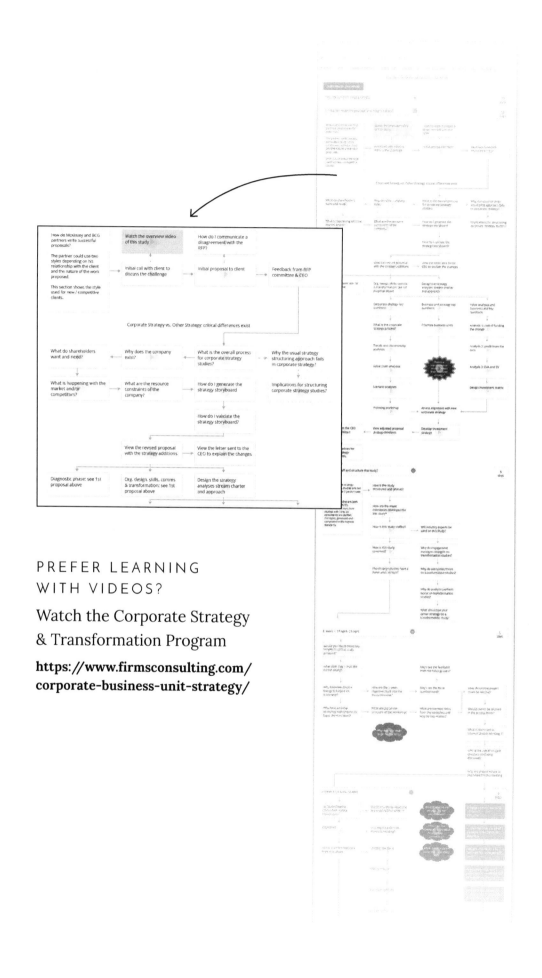

PREFER LEARNING WITH VIDEOS?

Watch the Corporate Strategy & Transformation Program

https://www.firmsconsulting.com/corporate-business-unit-strategy/

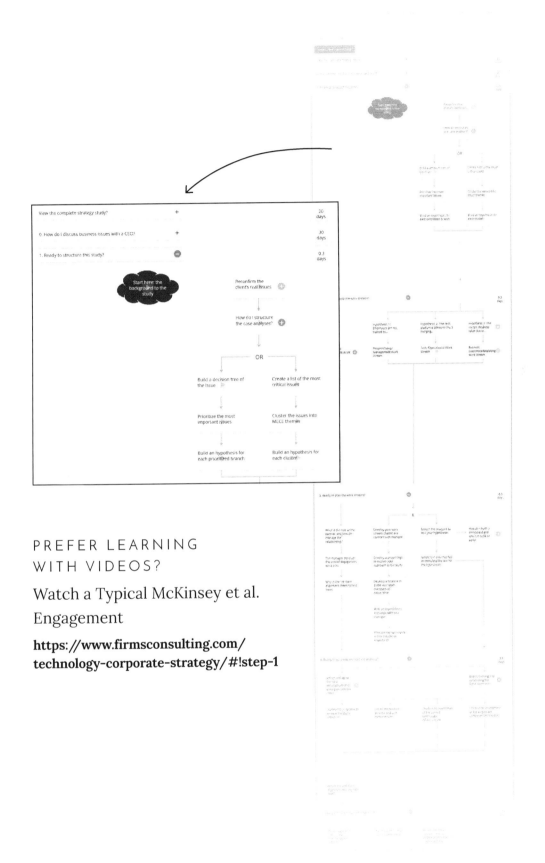

PREFER LEARNING WITH VIDEOS?

Watch a Typical McKinsey et al. Engagement

https://www.firmsconsulting.com/technology-corporate-strategy/#!step-1

ABOUT THE PUBLISHER

THE STRATEGY MEDIA GROUP

At the Strategy Media Group we believe in the power of critical thinking, creativity, and storytelling to teach our clients to solve mankind's toughest problems. Our mission is producing original long-form content to empower a loyal, hardworking, inspiring, well-meaning and ambitious worldwide audience to solve the most important problems and, as a result, make a positive and meaningful impact on the world.

Our clients make a difference because they aspire for more than what society had intended for them. They do not confuse aspiration for ambition. They choose the latter. They act.

We provide a full range of content development, financing, marketing and distribution services for wholly owned educational programs, documentaries, feature films, and podcasts teaching business strategy, problem-solving, critical thinking, communication, leadership and entrepreneurship streamed in >150 countries 24/7 through feature-rich Apps and websites.

At any given time >1,000 unpublished episodes are in post-production. Our digital properties include **StrategyTraining.com**, **StrategyTV.com** and **FirmsConsulting.com**. Our apps include Strategy Training, Strategy TV, Strategy Skills and Bill Matassoni A Memoir.

In addition, we own some of the world's most popular business strategy and case interview podcast channels with >4.5 million downloads and counting, and the world's largest business strategy OTT platforms with >6,000 episodes of original programming distributed on iOS, Android, Roku and Apple TV.

We have financed, packaged or distributed more than 45 premium programs through our wholly owned OTT platforms, including "The Electric Car Start-Up," "The Digital Luxury Atelier," "The Gold Miner," "Competitive Strategy with Kevin P. Coyne," "The Bill Matassoni Show," and we try to focus on social causes like championing the rights of disenfranchised workers.

We take an equity ownership positions in businesses we are documenting to produce programming for our platforms. Such as a gold miner, electric car start-up, luxury brands start-up, and new age cosmetics start-up.

THE STRATEGY JOURNAL

Our programming is analytically and conceptually deep, in that we dig into the numbers and details to help you understand the economics at work, and help you replicate our thinking. "The US Marketing Entry Study" and "The Corporate Strategy & Transformation Study," with >270 videos each, are programs used worldwide to understand the nuances of restructuring a retail bank and turning around a troubled power utility.

In the scripted space, we create original content combining education with entertainment to deliver business teachings.

Our publishing arm releases original books on strategy, business and critical thinking, such as "Marketing Saves the World" by Bill Matassoni, McKinsey's former senior partner and worldwide head of marketing, "Succeeding as a Management Consultant" and "Turquoise Eyes."

We teach business and critical thinking skills to children and young adults, with original and entertaining novels and programming merging entertainment and business training. We believe children and young adults will have a formidable advantage if they start learning to think like a strategy partner early in life. STEM skills should be complemented with critical reasoning skills. It should be strategy, science, technology, engineering and mathematics.

We invest in and have exposure to the world's fastest growing market segments and market geographies, including the BRICS. Our subscribers include senior government officials, and leaders of industry and consulting firms, all the way to the executive committee members of the world's leading consulting firms.

We work with eminent leaders such as ex-McKinsey, BCG et al. partners who plan, produce and/or host all our programming. The type of content we produce does not exist anywhere else in the world and is hosted exclusively on our platforms.

Kris Safarova is the Presiding Partner of Firmsconsulting.com, which owns the world's largest strategy streaming OTT channel. She works with a network of ex-McKinsey, BCG et al. partners to produce original strategy/leadership training programming and books. She manages several of the top podcast channels worldwide for strategy and management consulting, with >4.5 million downloads.

Kris Safarova was born in Samara City, the Russian Federation. She received a Dipl. in Music with a concentration in Classical Piano from DG Shatalov Music College, a B.Comm from UNISA, cum laude with highest distinction and an MBA from Ivey Business School, University of Western Ontario in Canada, on the dean's list with highest distinction, where she was President of the Public Sector Club and Editor of the Public Sector Journal. Prior to obtaining her business degrees, she worked in management consulting and post-MBA she was a banker and consulting engagement manager in Toronto, Canada. Prior to consulting Kris was a master classical concert pianist and official representative of the Russian Federation who toured Europe. She joined Firmsconsulting.com as a Partner, Corporate Finance in 2015 and was appointed Presiding Partner in 2016.

RECEIVE ACCESS TO EPISODES FROM OUR VARIOUS TRAINING PROGRAMS:

firmsconsulting.com/promo

GENERAL INQUIRIES:

support@firmsconsulting.com

COLLABORATION/PARTNERSHIP INQUIRIES:

kris@firmsconsulting.com

BULK ORDER REQUESTS/ GROUP MEMBERSHIPS:

support@firmsconsulting.com

SUGGEST A GUEST FOR OUR PODCAST CHANNELS:

support@firmsconsulting.com

Made in the USA
Middletown, DE
04 March 2022